Spiritual Verse Today
Heart and Soul
VOLUME II

SHARON CASSANOLOCHMAN

Copyright 2017 Sharon L. Lochman

ALL RIGHTS RESERVED. This book contains material protected under International and Federal Copyright Laws and Treaties. Any unauthorized reprint or use of this material is prohibited. No part of this book may be reproduced or transmitted in any form or by any means, electronic or mechanical, including photocopying, recording, or by any information storage and retrieval system without express written permission from the author/publisher.

Hardback
978-1-944878-82-5

Paperback
978-1-944878-95-5

Ebook
978-1-944878-83-2

Cover design by Debbie O'Byrne.

*To Don and Joan Foley—
Thank you for finding your way and helping
me to find mine.*

*Dedicated to the humble servants spreading God's Light—
the speakers, preachers, writers, and teachers.*

This is a work of fiction. Names, characters, events, and incidents either are the products of the author's imagination or used in a fictitious manner. Any resemblance to actual persons, living or dead, or actual events is purely coincidental.

Table of Contents

Faith *Never Forsaken* 1

Drifting to Monotony *Moments Unknown* 2

Coffee Grounds Spill to the Floor *Ordained Human* 3

Let Go *Release to God* 4

Judgements and Negativities *Goodness of Your Soul* 5

Suffering Souls *Speaking to the Heart* 6

Twist of Fate *Friendship's Sacred Phase* 7

Battlefields of Life *Comfort in God's Love* 8

Blessings Bestowed *Sanction Mind Wanderings* 9

Blessed to Call You Friend *Aho* 11

Found through Plight *Simply You*. 12

Battered and Worn *Replacing Strife* 13

Untidy Your Heart *Release from Sadness* 14

Bottom of the Glass *Believe in Yourself* 16

Nearing Journey's End *Compassionate Message* 18

Ragdoll Enthusiasm *Renew Faith in Yourself* 20

Heavenly Chore *Humble Servant* 21

Personal Connections *Freehand Goodbye* 22

Perfection to Your Core *Breath of God Gave Life* 23

Just Pray *Peace for All Nations* 25

Heart and Soul *Slippery Slope* 26

Limiting Experiences *Extend to Strangers* 28

Barnacle upon Her Side *The Earth is Alive* 29

Thorny Path *Healthier Fashion* 30

Gratitude to God *Universal Differences* 31

Each Day Forward *Prayer for a Friend* 32

Harshly Pointed Fingers *Peace in Your Life* 33

Loss of a Perfect Day *Joys of Youth* 34

Anchored to Shore *Facing the Unknown* 35

Borrower of Words *Gifted Talent* 36

Tendrils of Goodness *Spreading Gifts of Kindness* 38

Spiritual Verse Today: Heart and Soul

Shroud of Humanity *Courage* 39

Heart Shaken Free *Gifted Awareness* 40

High Expectations *Stress-Free* 41

Perfection of God's Love *Search Within* 42

Set Free *Vivid Colors* 44

Abandoned at Life's Gate *Dance* 45

Collective Whole *Whispers in the Wind* 46

Self-Sabotage *Writer's Block* 48

Unrelenting Pressure *Exhausting Distraction* 49

Political Persuasion *Spiritual Direction* 50

Anger Spilling *Peaceful Passage* 51

Dawn of a New Day *Let Go* 52

Search with Your Heart *Homeless and Compassion* 53

Cruel Host Dementia Plays *Peace and Patience* 54

Raindrops Haloed *Solid in Faith* 55

Unsteady Teeter *Spiritual Journey* 56

Faithful Life *Judgment Free* 57

Pray for Guidance *Uncertainties of Life* 58

Slice of a Sentence *Savor the Flavor* 59

Wasted Time *Windows of Life* 60

Strong in Faith *Life's Gate* 61

Angry Edge *Peace to Your Soul* 62

Forgiveness *Love from a Distance* 63

God's Voice *Roar of a Wave* 64

Happiness Gifted *Seeker* 65

Earth Day *Cascading the Globe* 66

Misplaced Ideals *Grandness of Character* 67

Love Gifted *Harm to None* 68

Forgotten Sensations *Wakeful Joy* 69

God's Gift *Second Chances* 70

Troubling Time *Embrace Light* 71

Universal Suffering *Let God* 72

Heavenly Design *Your Calling* 73

Assumptions and Judgements *Shoes of Another* 74

Days Tally *Walk with God* 75

Forgiveness Knot *Live Life Forward* 76

Stillness of You *Intentions Heard* 77

Gifted another Day *Give Gratitude* 78

Toxic Relationship *Gate Locked and Sealed* 79

Shield of Laughter *Realize Your Worthiness* 80

Spiritual Verse Today: Heart and Soul

Let Your Light Shine *Worthy a Beautiful Life* 81

Loneliness *Strands of a Web* 82

Life Gifted *Nature's Toll* 83

Verses Songs Paintings *Spread Goodwill* 84

Unsettled Within *God's Embrace* 85

Strength of Humanity *Diversity in Light* 86

Spiritual Ladder *Upward Looking* 87

Heart Still Broken *Delicacy of Life* 88

Anger Vulnerability Sorrow *Step into God's Light* 89

Honor Life Gifted *Heavenly Connection* 90

Believe *Shadow Cast* 91

Life Eternal *Promised by God* 92

Tormented Existence *Courage to Stand Tall* 93

Actions of One *God's Breath* 94

Clover to Buttercups *High Expectations* 95

Shoes of Another *Spiritual Ladder* 96

Society's Neglect *Heaven's Light* 97

Today is for Living *Teapot Screams* 98

Weight of the World *Butterfly Graces* 100

A Miracle Bestowed *Depths of Sadness* 101

Path Taken *Heavenly Direction* 103

Life Lived Full *Laughter Heard* 104

Mother's Day *Share Bread* 105

Teetering Direction *Pray* 106

Rough Spots Traveled *Patience and Love* 107

Shadows beneath Familiar Faces *White Doves* 108

Waste Not *Follow God's Light* 109

Battle the Page *Let Your Words Bloom* 110

Weighted Existence *Cleanse* 111

Crooked Choices *Better Tomorrow* 112

Attention-Getting Behavior *Good of the Whole* 113

Grace *Smallest of Shoes* 114

Sheltering the Blows *Light against Shore* 115

Battles Fought *Peace Deprived* 116

Traffic of Life *Blessings to You* 117

Measure of Worth *Preacher Teacher Speaker Writer* 118

Grief *God's Light* 120

Frailty of Heart *Laborer of God* 121

Friendship Embraced *Purity of Love* 122

Ravaging Cells *Prayers to You* 123

Spiritual Verse Today: Heart and Soul

Glory of God *Joining of Hearts*.................... 124

Awakening *Forgiveness Relieved* 125

Raging Anger *Fear Manifested* 126

God's Gifted Breath *Reconciliation*................ 127

Sing through Words *Rainbow Colored Pages* 128

Prayers Gifted from Compassion *Unity of Hearts* 129

Smoldering Ash of Light *Flame Eternal* 130

Shackled Memories *Internal Harmony* 131

Integrity Honesty Humility *Riches to Possess*......... 132

Surrender to Your Sorrow *Woundedness* 133

One Foot Flat *Spirit of God's Light*................ 135

Joyful Living *God Gifted* 136

God's Gift *Blessings and Breath*................... 137

Violence *Take Faith*........................... 138

Challenges of Grief *Face another Day*.............. 139

Social Media and Heartbreak *Great Divide*........... 140

Words Knotted *A Nightingale's Song*............... 141

Unfolding of Life *Patience Faith Strength* 142

Death's Darkness *Sorrowful Loss*.................. 143

Used Furniture and Chipped Porcelain Sinks
Sturdy Stance........................... 144

Mending the Broken Heart *Love and Affection* 145

Just Pray! *Shine Brighter*...................... 146

Faith and God's Light *Shadows of Life* 147

Home with God *Flickering Light* 148

Compassion Spoken *Lighting the Way*............... 149

Stand United *Humbled by Grace*.................. 150

Pain Carefully Tendered *Cloud of Commotion*.......... 151

Imagine *Believe*............................ 152

Dead-Ended Decisions *Gentle Direction*.............. 153

Healing Forgiveness *Life Changing*................. 154

Passage of Time *Holiday Sorrows* 155

Overcome the Past *Step into Today*................ 156

Political Agendas *Times of Challenge*............... 157

Violence and Drama *Prayers to the Universe* 158

Author's Note

We walk not alone on this journey called life—this path of intersecting souls. Each heart linked through the breath gifted from the Father. We are the speakers, teachers, writers, and preachers.
The actions of one greatly affect the whole.

—**Sharon CassanoLochman**

FAITH
Never Forsaken

I see you at the gate of great happenings. A universe of miraculous events and experiences await each new day. But there you are, clinging to fear. Afraid to let go. Afraid to soar. My friend, what holds you in place?

Are you afraid to be a dreamer without dreams? A writer without a pen? A lover without love? A parent without children? A singer without a voice? An instrument that cannot play?

My friend, happiness and dreams realized are but one-step away. God walks by your side through all life experiences. Times of abundance and times of tears. Stop clinging to fear and take His hand. Follow the gentle and loving direction every step of every day. Sing loudly. Write freely. Love openly. For the circle in which you sit is vast and humbling. For the circle in which you sit is all that is needed.

Allow life to fall into place with faith.

DRIFTING TO MONOTONY
Moments Unknown

I've watched for a while. Headway made across turbulent waters. Calm in sight. Then pulling in the oars. Drifting to monotony. What is it that pulls you to shore?

Fear? Fear of what? The unknown? Is not each new step taken, one-step forward you've not taken before? Fear of success? Why do you doubt the talents you've been gifted? You do not serve God's highest intention by lowering your potential.

Fear not the power you hold. Fear not your path. Fear not challenges or successes. You are worthy of so much more. Man your boat. Paddle from shore.

Great are your gifts. Believe in yourself and in the powers you hold.

You have a purpose. Forward on. Sail to new and open waters. Joyfully live in each new moment unknown.

COFFEE GROUNDS SPILL TO THE FLOOR

Ordained Human

Pacing the floor, angst fills your moments. Shame and sorrow. One secret gifted to a friend sent sailing on the wind from one chattering voice to the listening ears of another.

Coffee grounds spill to the floor, scattering in every direction.

They found you out.

You're human.

Were you born into this world all knowing? Were you born gifted with a ridged and straight path lacking free choice and variation? Or were you born an innocent and perfect child destined to learn from your mistakes and environment?

My friend, you were born an ordained human.

Let the coffee grounds spill to the floor.

Your evidence of humanity merely accentuates the power of a peaceful awakening. Your evidence of humanity merely accentuates the power of learning and personal growth.

Keep close those that recognize your beauty. Keep close those that do not rally in the pain and suffering of others. Keep close those that walk in God's Light for they can see beyond the coffee grounds scattered upon the floor.

LET GO
Release to God

I share your dilemma. Matters not the age or reason. They tug gently at first to find their space.

You had to let go.

Tearfully you watched as their fingertips released from your hold. So quickly they grow. Pulling away. Why didn't you keep more? Memories and trinkets. Artwork taped to the refrigerator door. You miss holding them. Tucking them in and *I love you more*. Clinging soft arms. Purity and innocence.

It's time.

Release them back into the fold. Worry not they'll be lost among the marching steps of sleeping souls. They'll never be alone. Guided and protected with God's heavenly hold, until they can march independently on their own.

Gift to God your precious cargo once carried to cross the streets through the turbulent traffic of intersecting souls. May they always be nudged in the highest direction.

Gift to them this life journey by letting go.

JUDGEMENTS AND NEGATIVITIES

Goodness of Your Soul

Smile I do within my heart. Your searching has begun. Awake, dear one. Awake. Change of the mindset now in order. The popular belief you live like a heathen. Partier, negotiator of reason. Wonder *they* do, who are *you* that transpires to climb the spiritual ladder? Obstacles and temptations. Judgements and negativities abound.

Change of the mindset of one is all that is required. You are already a spiritual soul. Powerful in the goodness of your core. Easier to be that which God has intended. Full of grace. Peaceful. Happy. Spreading truth and joy.

Simply be yourself. Child of God—hop back on the ladder.

SUFFERING SOULS

Speaking to the Heart

It is not the gurus, mystics, psychics, or preachers to which I speak. It is to the suffering and wandering souls that seek. Seeking kindness and attention from another human being. Lifting of the consciences or spirits from this moment to the next. Speaking to the heart of those alone or lost within. Lean on my borrowed words until the balance has resumed. Then stand on your own.

Life is a cycle of ups and downs. Tally not deeds done. But rally together. Togetherness is the key to a life of success. For alone we are never when we walk in Light.

Gifted to you with prayerful wishes, a day of peaceful reflection. Passed then on to a stranger. A love connection from your sacred heart-place. For it is from there which I speak. I gift to you love universal.

TWIST OF FATE

Friendship's Sacred Phase

Sorry for your twist of fate. Once a gifted speaker. Linguistics now forgotten. Paralyzed of words. Paralyzed of phrases. Movement resigned to angular motions. Good-bye I have said to our friendship as I've known it. But say good-bye to you, dear one, I will not.

Even through this twist of fate, I see your Light. Chatter on and on I will. One-sided through lost memories and vacant stares. But really, one-sided it is not. For I hear with my heart all you wish to share.

Promise I have from God that when our earthly journey ends, life continues. Run you shall through meadows, healthy once again. Holding my hand and heart in laughter. Stories shared.

Until that time comes to pass, anchored to your bedside I remain. Gifting words to fill your head. Friendship's sacred phase. For behind the blankness resides my friend.

BATTLEFIELDS OF LIFE

Comfort in God's Love

A battle wages on. Shackled to your ankle are the memories of war and human strife. The body yearns for what the mind will not release. Sleep. Night terrors repeat. Unsavory sights to gentle eyes. Guilt for those left behind.

My friend, you were called to action. An unnatural request to which the human persona is not well equipped. Tragic on all counts. Horrific pain remains. Memories of war weigh heavily on your heart.

Release your pain to God. Release the unrelenting emotional cycles that reign over day and night. Seek solace in the comfort of God's love. Triumph over shackled memories of war and human strife. Triumph by living life.

With each breath may you be filled with God's Light.

Gratitude I give for your service to our country. Prayers I send that you may walk free from the memories that weigh so heavily upon your heart. Blessings to you, my friend. You are not alone. God is at your side.

BLESSINGS BESTOWED

Sanction Mind Wanderings

I am saddened you see life as a challenge. Your body is calm as your mind races. Caught in a cycle pondering life's greatest quests but easily interrupted by the escapades of a wayward ant. Frustrated you wish for a head void of rambling thoughts and awkward delays. You pray for conformity, tranquility, and an end to the relentless strife for a simpler way.

You are right. You are not the same.

You carry within your core the vision of inventions, untold stories, solutions to problems. Society challenges the mind that leaps. *Sit down! Sit still! Don't think!* Following directions is not your forte. Multiple-choice life questions or fragmented directives leave your mind wandering—back to the wayward ant.

But what of the greatest of the great, pondering the stars and universe. Societal norms were more likely a challenge for them as well.

The mind you wish to dull is indeed the greatest asset for the whole. Dream on. Think on. Sanction mind wandering. Explore the planets, great works, and instruments Divine. Ponder your existence. Reality. Your life. Ponder mine. Ponder the wandering ant.

You are not the same.

You are a blessing.

See the gift bestowed upon you, not as an earthly harness—but the Universe's wings to take flight. Let your mind ramble. Everything will fall into place. The tension you feel is the straight jacket *they've* placed—corralling your mind for a mass-produced race.

Far better to ponder the unknowns, than to live an assembly-line existence of the cute and conformed. Matched in their heads. Matched in their homes. No variation. No thoughts of their own. Programmed like their favorite television shows. They are sleeping—dreaming of cruises, cars, and fat dollars.

My dear one, you are not the same. Your calling is spectacular. Your mind is magnificent. Follow the mental chaos. The more you let go, the less your mind will race.

You were put here to learn and play. Nothing wrong with your wrap. You're one of God's children in a most precious and positive way.

Have the courage to follow the wayward ant. Follow the journey of unanswered questions. Cure cancer. Write an opera. Dance with emotion and grace. Investigate.

Please, do not wish God's most precious gift away.

Walk proudly. Lift your head to the Heavens and recognize the blessings bestowed upon you. Heel to toe, heel to toe, and heel to toe. Follow the wayward ant to the paths unknown.

BLESSED TO CALL YOU FRIEND

Aho

So blessed am I to call you friend. Tenderer of the many. Healer to all. Confident and strong. Attributes required for the burden for which you've been called.

Aho for your efforts. *Aho* for your strength. *Aho* for the Light you carry within. *Aho* for believing in me when I, and all else, failed to see. *Aho* for leading, believing, and guiding wandering souls and me.

So blessed am I for you my friend.

FOUND THROUGH PLIGHT

Simply You

Under a rock was revealed a personality worth a fight. It belongs to you. Found though plight. You are yourself. Occasionally slow to speak. Tripping over misconstrued intentions. Hesitant beyond belief. But, dear one, it is simply you. Permitted you are to take time. Decisions weighing and swaying from left to right. Timid and shy.

Underneath the rock of debris of hurtful actions from others stands a soul ready to take flight. Stand strong in the knowledge of the goodness you carry. Trust in yourself in times of struggle. Trust in God for paths taken.

Let your Light shine as the wondrous creation known as you. Incredibly glorious. You are worth the fight. *Fight for your Light.* Let it shine.

BATTERED AND WORN
Replacing Strife

I sense the distraction and unrest. Caught you are between the waves and sharp rocks of life. Tossed about. Battered and worn. Weary. Beat.

Take a moment to self-reflect. Sit for a while. Recognize the path that has brought you to this place. Lift your tear-stained face to God. Bring to God the sadness carried within. Travel forward in a most positive way. Look for the signs. Peace and joy replacing strife.

Gift your burdens to God. Allow God's abundance in your life.

UNTIDY YOUR HEART
Release from Sadness

Helplessly I watch as you carry yourself on a sea of sadness, floating away from life's most precious moments.

Untidy your heart. Scatter and dismiss those things that feed your sadness. Toss life's negativities to the breeze. Release self-indulging and self-destroying memories that keep you from life's destiny. Memories you covet through fear. Fear of hurt, judgment, shame, or loss. Buried and neatly organized in your most sacred place. Memories deposited from your head to your heart.

Tidy and neatly organized compartments stand ready for a mental or emotional battle. *I remember when*, as you pull from one compartment or another. *I'll never let that happen again.* You hide behind your earthly façade of false notions and false emotions. False emphasis on what is truly important.

But wait, what are you missing through your clouded, tearful vision? Could this be a good experience, a life lesson, a moment of brightness now denied to your soul?

Imagine yourself with closed eyes and hands tied behind your back. Imagine finding your way through life with the guidance of your heart and the knowledge that comes forth from within. Imagine floating on a rainbow-colored sea of hope, peace, and serenity, enjoying the moment. Enjoying life without fear. Enjoying the solely wondrous anticipation of what is yet to come.

Imagine today, this moment—finding the serenity of the moment through your heart.

BOTTOM OF THE GLASS
Believe in Yourself

I have missed you. I have missed our conversations. Quiet moments spent in silly laughter. Sharing dreams and hopes. Embracing life together.

I have missed *you*.

I see you but have not *seen* you for a while.

What is it that you run from as you sink to the bottom of the glass? Swishing and twisting bitter tastes of life's memories. You turn to the glass to deaden the past. But in turn, the glass dead-ends you.

What chases you from within? Self-inflicted thoughts generated from interpretations, experiences, and lost expectations? Manifested demons whilst your soul cries from within.

My dear one, run not. Stand strong and face that which you cast into the hazy darkness at the bottom of the glass. Face your realities, not through clouded vision, but through the Light. Stand with God. Stand tall.

You carry within the strength to face life's challenges. You are so much stronger than you think.

Believe in yourself. Believe in God. Allow God to carry you until you can carry on alone.

There is so much more to life. There is so much more to you. You are missing life, and I miss you.

NEARING JOURNEY'S END
Compassionate Message

Sadness fills your sleepless nights as you carry the burden of your family's loss heavily in your heart. Your search for comfort cannot be realized through the limited confines of your earthly existence.

You're tired.
Tired of pretending.
Tired of being all for all.
Tired of illness waging war within your frail body.
Tired.

You long, once again, for the childlike embrace of your mother's arms—yearning for her words of wisdom and comfort. Take note, dear one, your mother is with you. She tends your soul, gently nudging you towards life's final escapade.

Your body fails as man and medicine have reached an end to their limited interventions. Your body fails, but your spirit is strong. Step back and away from your earthly vessel.

I love you. I wish in your final hour, to let go. . . .

Let go and soar through the Heavens on the wings of angels. Set yourself free from illness, heartache, disappointment, pain, and the harsh realities of this journey known as life. Search deep within the caverns of your earthly memories, taking savored moments of beauty and grace with you to Heaven's gate.

You have given the world many lessons of life. You have lived to the fullest. I wish peace for your body. I wish freedom for your soul.

I will miss you.

RAGDOLL ENTHUSIASM

Renew Faith in Yourself

Sorry to see that you wear life. Furrowed brows. Expression etched with despair. Ragdoll enthusiasm. Dragging through one day to the next. My friend, there are no guarantees from one moment to the next. Look not to the negatives, but to the gifts.

Gratitude given for the gift of a new day. Shattered dreams replaced or renewed. Pick up. Look up. Inhale God's graces. Strength will prevail. This earth walk is shorter than you think. Waste not one moment with self-pity. You are here for a reason. Look to the good you can do.

Renew faith in yourself. Expand abilities and possibilities. Offer compassion and good tidings. Impossible to portage dark emotions when focusing on the needs of another; many suffer far greater than you.

Look for blessings gifted each day. Be a blessing to another.

HEAVENLY CHORE
Humble Servant

I grasp your burden so gracefully carried. A heavenly chore to uplift the spirits of the many.

May you remain a humble servant. Aware of the needy. Prepared to share. Gifted much and gifting back to the many. Always remembering for the collaborative good of the whole. May God's compassion reflect from you back to the Universe tenfold.

A beacon of God's Light may you remain. Steadfast in the need to uplift the spirits of the many. Lest you forget . . . your burden will never be too heavy with heavenly support.

PERSONAL CONNECTIONS

Freehand Goodbye

What's happened to this society of ours? Mechanical devices limiting personal connections. Misunderstood messaging. Typing and tapping. Vanished are facial expressions. Happy faces now sent with single-digit intentions. Experiencing nature through mixed media.

Preference should be to simply look up. Boycott the artificial sunrise. Wake early. Take within the out-of-doors. Constantly changing are the visual effects. Those in nature and that of a friend.

Look not to a screen or hold a phone to your ear. Make time for a personal visit. Speak your intentions. Deposit to memory a genuine smile. Share soothing recollections of the gifted new day. Bond with the emotions of heartfelt recollections.

When the time for departure calls, opt-out from toots, beeps, and chimes. Try an old-fashioned freehand wave goodbye.

PERFECTION TO YOUR CORE

Breath of God Gave Life

You are a rock.

Rough-surfaced from nature's tribulations. Dotted with darkened hues contrasted by Light. Tossed and turned. Molded by the elements of life.

Like a rock you once were. From the earth you came. Breath of God gave life.

No longer resembling that which you once were. The elements have changed you. Rough, cracked, and worn. You could not control your molding any more than the rock.

Waste time no longer looking to the past with sadness or anger. It was. You are. Regardless of the elements. Rise above life challenges. Learn to be. Learn to see. See the perfection carried within.

The rock is still the rock in all its manipulation. The core remains the same. *Smash it,* you say, as life has smashed you. *Shatter it to a million pieces.* But each piece still holds perfection to the core. Regardless of size or dimension. Likewise for you. Regardless of how many times your heart has been broken; how many times you've been hurt by another; how many times you've look for, wanted, or needed—your core is still perfection.

Beautiful, loving perfection. Look within. See what God sees. Your core.

JUST PRAY

Peace for All Nations

Our conversations of late drift to a negative sort. Hopeless you appear for the troubled world in which we live. Difference of opinion if I may speak. Transformation of energy is pending along the horizon of life. The actions we take will carry to future generations. United in prayer a possible solution.

Pray for yourself. Pray for the world. Pray for the planet coughing and wheezing from spewed man-made debris. United we can stand within contrary beliefs. You can be you. I can be me. Together linked with hearts and praying hands.

Pray for all souls. Pray for miracles to those that go without. Wrap the earth in positive affirmations. Listen to prayerful reminders angelically placed. The smile of a baby. A gentle sunrise greeting each new day. Pray for unity and peace for all nations. Matters not color, religion, or location. Brothers and sisters united together can make a difference.

Just pray.

HEART AND SOUL
Slippery Slope

Dear one, in such a rush you have been as of late. Unable to talk. Time better spent, or so you thought. Fisted knuckles white and tense. Clinging to the rungs of society's ladder.

To what avail awaits? Known in and amongst the most popular of people? Dining and vacationing above and beyond? Is it a ladder to which you cling or a slippery slope of insignificant chatter? Fool's gold blown to the wind.

Better to be remembered for acts of kindness than the ski slopes of Colorado. Better to be remembered not at all, than to have passed on the opportunity to take the trail of life's purpose.

Issues there are not for a *place* amongst the divinely self-appointed. Dining and vacationing are but pleasures meant to be enjoyed—not gathered.

Climb the ladder, spiritually speaking. Each rung a reminder of lessons learned and distance traveled. Time better spent on this moment. Recognizing old friends. Sitting within to study one's internal navigations. Set your compass north. Set your life expectations high. Be all. See all. Do all. Give wholly of heart and soul to your life journey and Earth Mother. Child of God, live life to the fullest because it is *your* purpose, not a rung climbed on a social ladder.

LIMITING EXPERIENCES

Extend to Strangers

Closed off you are. Living within the confines of the family. Segregated from society. Managing life with circular vision. Limiting experiences. Coerced reality. Missing life's meaning.

Look beyond the confines of four walls. Ignorance and ignoring will not enhance the human race. Extending and embracing will make the difference. Extend to strangers gentle gestures. A nod or smile. Acknowledge their existence. Look to their uniqueness with open vision. See the Light carried within. And when you are ready—offer conversation. Many parallel experiences will surface when willing to listen.

Embrace the differences from one person to the next. Go outside of yourself and your circular vision. Beyond superficial and learned inhibitions. For at this moment you may experience the awesome joy of human connection.

BARNACLE UPON HER SIDE

The Earth is Alive

Can't you feel it? The sweet breath and heartbeat of our planet. This place we call home. The rock beneath our heavily trudging feet. Substance giver of life.

We live as a barnacle upon her side.

Our path is intertwined with Earth Mother. She is alive. Carefully tending the water we drink. The soil that reaps. The air we breathe.

Walk gently. Don't run. Respect paid to the delicacy of this place. Harmony required for her survival as well as our own. Make one change today. One change to save this sacred place called home.

One change today. Then perhaps again tomorrow. Take that talked about walk instead of the drive. Opt for glass instead of plastic. Recycle. Pint-size changes compounded by millions will make the difference.

Harmony required to coexist. One change today is such a small sacrifice to save our sacred place called home.

THORNY PATH

Healthier Fashion

So easily it happens. Distractions of a harmful sort. Hanging around the corner post of another. Wishing for. Wanting. Waiting for *their* momentary discontent. Planning your move. Stepping in. Stepping out. So much unnecessary restlessness. Let the two make their way together or apart.

Look elsewhere for distraction. Make another choice. Fill heart space in a healthier fashion. Busy yourself. Reconnect with nature. Reconnect with you. Idle heart and idle mind leave space for crooked travel down a thorny trail.

Choices in this life we will always have. Focus on the highest of goals and thorny obstacles will become a thing of the past.

GRATITUDE TO GOD

Universal Differences

So testy and agitated you are of late. Impatient and belittling of strangers and friends. Attitude towards choices *they make*. How to talk, walk, dress, and eat. So much time wasted questioning and judging the actions and decisions of others. Stop trying to remold them like you. Allow for dignity in differences.

Look at what you deem as a fault, but more as a gift from above. Uniqueness is God's specialty. Look closely at the Universe. Are we not as different as garden arrangements?

Needed are procrastinating dreamers to see life through visions. Needed are take-charge doers birthing visions to action. Needed are nitpicking detailers delivering action to fruition. Needed are kind-hearted souls bridging the gap.

Balancing energies is embracing humanity. Each person on this planet has their place. Thanks to God—we are *not* the same. Look at the differences with joy and compassion. Pick up the slack and honor their gift as well as your own.

Dream—do—think—connect. It will be for the greater good of all.

EACH DAY FORWARD

Prayer for a Friend

May you find peace, safety, protection, joy, and love in all that you see and do.

May you live to behold beauty and miracles of many levels and degrees.

May anger and fear be replaced with love, understanding, and compassion.

May God guide you to peace and tranquility.

May you live each day forward in harmony with the Universe.

HARSHLY POINTED FINGERS

Peace in Your Life

My sympathies for the drama you face. So harshly they point fingers. Straight to your face they will never say, but behind your back they are quick to lash.

But words have a way of circling. Traveling forth. Deposited righteously upon your front door.

My friend, the severity towards you is *their* inability to look within.

Stand tall. Say, *thanks*. Thanks for the reminder of where you have been. Thanks for the reminder of things you have done. Thanks for the reminder of who you were and who you proudly have become.

You are a person of great personal growth. Hard lessons learned. Personal battles fought. You've looked within, and come out on top.

Forget the drama! Seek peace in your life. Tranquility. Simply say, *thanks*.

LOSS OF A PERFECT DAY

Joys of Youth

It rained today. So sad were you for the intrusion. The loss of a perfect day.

Stop.

Look within. Look out. Were not the soft hues of darkening clouds glorious? Was not the fresh drink of water released to the Earth a miracle? Look not to God's miracle with negative connotations. Look to the miracle with the wonder and excitement of a child. Look to the miracle of rain for that which it is—a blessing.

Forget the tedious restrictions of maturity that bind you indoors. Don old clothing—the play clothes of youth. Puddle jump in God's miracle. Puddle jump for the child within. Forget not the simple joys of your youth. Get wet. Get muddy. Play.

Then thank God for the beautiful day.

ANCHORED TO SHORE

Facing the Unknown

What holds you anchored to shore? Life pounding. Tears flowing. Hunched forward. Head bowed. Afraid to let go of the rocky cliff ledge. Easier you think to adapt to what is known. Riding out storms. Crying silently from the bottom of your soul.

My friend, fear consumes your ability to see. To see your potential and strength. Your worthiness of love and abundance in life. To feel God's Light. Cut free of the unwarranted fears hindering happiness. For in God's graces you will never go without.

Set yourself free. Free of fear. Push off. Float majestically in the peace and calm of being. Sometimes the most peaceful journey is shore-free.

BORROWER OF WORDS

Gifted Talent

Borrower of words. Giving life to thoughts and phrases. Misspelling. Inventing new definitions. Molding for sound knowing the rest will work out later.

Borrower of words. Painter upon the mind's canvas. Splattering images laced with savory flavors. Spinning adventures. Touching hearts. Lifting the souls of many.

Borrower of words, your talents are greatly needed.

Borrower of words. Look to what God has so generously gifted. Gaze not with malice upon the page crafted. See creativity at its finest. Know you write for a reason. Allow the words to trail from the pen to paper . . . finding their place in hearts and imaginations.

Borrower of words. Writing is not a tedious journey but an exciting expedition of time and unearthly voyages. Walk through sky-high flowing grasses. Ride on the back of an eagle. Soar to the Heavens. Become the voice of a child. Put to paper for those without vision.

Borrower of words. You hold the key to the imagination. Fear not your gifted talent. Play at your craft. Tedious it is not to join your characters upon paper. Love their antics. Love their personalities. Give life to their surroundings. Layer language with color. Look not to compare with the craft of the aged. Release your gifted voice . . . even when coming from a different direction.

Borrower of words. Romp joyfully on the playground God has provided. Set your attitude in a positive place. Passionately play at your craft. Skip across pages.

Borrower of words. Splash the world with your colored thoughts and phrases. Orchestrate sounds and smells. Worry not for publication. The rest will work out later.

TENDRILS OF GOODNESS

Spreading Gifts of Kindness

Troubled you are with man's chosen destiny. Programming bombarded with negativity. Is there no space, on the air or in reality, for the goodness that still exists?

We are all floating amidst the darkness of lost souls. Look not to the dark but the glory of the whole. We have such potential. Turn your actions to the betterment for all.

Start small. Open a door. Simply say, *hello*.

One kind word planted in the heart of another. See how it grows. Tendrils of goodness seeking God's Light.

Natural gifts of kindness are contagious. Infect mankind with the seed of kindness. The seed you plant today can alter the destiny of man's tomorrow.

Kindness is free to give. Priceless to the receiver.

SHROUD OF HUMANITY

Courage

Surely there's more to life than watching the escapades of others. Wasted moments, wringing your hands. Hostage to your home. Hostage to life.

You live your life like that of a mouse. Timid and afraid. Scampering from window to window peeking through life's blinds. Easier to look out than to look within.

It takes courage to live an earthly life. Courage, my friend.

Set your intention in motion. Monumental leaps will abound if you take the first step. Step out of yourself. Cast aside that which once was—a mannequin covered in the shroud of humanity.

One small step, my friend. Lift your heart to the Heavens. Do not focus on the could-have-been. Focus on the now. Make a difference in this world. Make a difference for you.

Look inward. Look upward. Look to fill your heavy heart with love, compassion, joy, and happiness. Look to God. Mind not the actions of others. Take action with yourself.

Smile. Be happy. Step out of yourself and into God's Light.

HEART SHAKEN FREE
Gifted Awareness

My heart sings. Happy I am for your latest plight. The distress carried comes from a heart shaken free. Awakening you are to the Oneness with all creations. Time to rejoice. Compassion fills the heart's shadowed areas, forcing sorrow and shame to spill out. The sudden awareness of the hurtful actions conveyed to others. Overwhelming for a while. Sit with yourself. Sit with your life.

Lean against the porcelain sink. Wash away tainted memories. Cleanse your heart. Ask for forgiveness. Then forgive yourself.

It is not the intention to forever be beaten by replaying actions and situations. It is the intention to move forward with growth spiritual in nature. Learn and don't repeat. That was then. This is now.

Rejoice, my friend, for you are awake. Take in God's breath. Fear and aloneness now replaced with Oneness. Welcome to God's love and compassion.

It can be a challenging time. Awareness of yourself, your actions, and your connection to the Universe. Peace to you through your spiritual journey.

HIGH EXPECTATIONS
Stress-Free

So many expectations set in stone. Easy to fail. With Light in your heart, life arranges easier. Playful tendencies positive in nature obliterates the word *failure*. Life was gifted to be enjoyed. Lessons become less painful—stress-free.

Live in Light through actions and words. Approach obligations with the highest of intentions. Joyfully reach goals and live dreams. Enjoy life. Smile through disappointments, which are truly blessings in disguise. For you will be successful in endeavors when you joyfully seek.

PERFECTION OF GOD'S LOVE
Search Within

I understand the place from which you come. You walk through life in darkness, fenced among humanity yet alone with the vision of a blind man. Your life full, surrounded by friends and family. Busy you are, morning to night. Busy with good tidings and earthly accomplishments. But you find yourself yearning for more. Yearning for clarity and understanding of that which is grander. Grander than the last promotion. Grander than a baby's first breath.

Crazy, you think to yourself. What else can there be? What else, separate from that which you know? Separate from this which you live. Day-to-day. This. Simple. Basic. Existence.

But, dear one, there *is* more. There is more to life. More to you. More than accomplishments. More than promotions, bigger houses, and better cars.

There's you.

You are the grandest of that which is. You.

You are the perfection of God's love. Peace, serenity, and joy.

Search no more, for you simply need to open your eyes. Look within yourself. Humbly acknowledge the beauty and purity of your soul. God created you. God gave you breath.

Find peace, dear friend. Find peace within your soul.

SET FREE
Vivid Colors

You stand invisible against the papered wall. Dusty yellowed hues like that of a vintage movie. Quietly watching a world full of people. Wishing to be heard but afraid to be noticed.

It is a lonely place. You were meant to be more.

More does not entail vulgarity or aggressive behavior. More does not entail narcissistic demands on others. More entails being yourself. Whatever the definition is of you. Step into yourself. Boldly hued colors adorn your essence. You are light and sound in harmony with the planet. Not the backdrop behind someone else's podium.

It is a disservice to all of humanity to hide behind dusty yellowed hues. For you are a gift. Kind and compassionate. Sensible and forgiving. A lover of all of God's creations. You are uniquely you.

Shine your vivid colors for all the world to see. Worry not for those too blind with themselves to notice. The rest of the world will benefit when you step forward.

ABANDONED AT LIFE'S GATE

Dance

So consumed are you with that which devours time with scurry. Head spinning whilst life spins out of control.

Your inner child, full of innocence and joy, sits abandoned at life's gate.

Stop, my friend. Stop for a mere moment. Go to a safe place sequestered from watchful eyes. Lift up your arms to the Heavens and give thanks for your life. Then dance. Dance in the darkness until you're able to dance in the Light.

Your child from within is knocking at the gate. Let in the child. Let in the Light.

You are *still* a child of God's. You are *still* full of life, love, and innocence—if you will just open the gate.

COLLECTIVE WHOLE

Whispers in the Wind

The Universe awaits. Go forth without fear, for courage and strength run through your very essence—despite the defiance etched into the grains and furrows of your brow. You are an old soul, plucked from the Heavens to forge goodness and love along your path. Not for personal glory or wealth, and not for greed, but for the collective whole of humanity.

The Heavens await the feast of peaceful vibrations gathering energy through the surge.

Look to the positive of the moment. The beauty of today. The wonders of now. Ground yourself in nature. Look not with your eyes, but with your heart. Trust your heart for a clarity of vision. See the true beauty in its simplest form. Let the tears flow as you recognize pure magnificence.

Harm to no soul. That is your one commandment. Harm to no soul for we are of the same breath. Reach with your heart and feel the heavenly energy that surrounds.

You are me—I am you.

You awake, eyes still crusted with sleep as you strain for clarity through the haze of life. You have been gifted nature at its best. Learn to see these gifts. They are everywhere. How many moments have you missed because you could not see through sleep-laden eyes? These were donations from Heaven. Gifts from your soul to lighten your journey. Step out of your earthly body. Learn to listen to whispers in the wind.

Time to awaken from *reality* and step into your heavenly dream. Be grateful for all souls passed and intersected along your journey. The change will come in the form of peace and tranquility.

Safe travels.

SELF-SABOTAGE
Writer's Block

Motivation and talent are not in question. Struggle you do needlessly. Writer's block or self-sabotage? Unduly and worrisome misgivings.

Clear your head of self-imposed directives. Write from your heart. Write with your God-given talent. There are as many word combinations as colors to fill the sunset sky. Take from the palette of emotions drawn from life.

When that doesn't work—disconnect. Move to the side. Stop blocking progress. Let the pen's GPS find the route across the page. Think not, for the more you think the less you will write.

Have faith in yourself. Trust in the process. Visualize God painting the sky good night. Swatches of gray-blue blending oranges with whites. Endless array. Never the same. So will be your writing if you'll just get out of the way.

UNRELENTING PRESSURE

Exhausting Distraction

So much to do. Unrelenting pressure. Straining to do all and be all. A spinning cycle, faster and faster. Life is short. To that, I agree. But joyful existence was God's intention. Approach life with the innocence of youth. Shift gears from fast forward. The speed in which you travel should be natural. God will provide the tempo and challenges. What is. Everything else will be. Live with tears of joy minus the exhausting distractions.

When living in the moment, all that is gathered is purest of intention. Grueling tasks become a pleasure. Check in on long-term goals. But live not with future expectations or where you have already gone. Storms will continue to rest along the horizon. But balanced you will remain without fear when in the moment.

Let go of the strain. Permit yourself to live simply. Joyfully approach obligations and notions. Trust in the guidance and help from God. Release stressful incantations. You are already wonderfully blended.

POLITICAL PERSUASION

Spiritual Direction

Foggy is your spiritual direction. Hidden beneath. Personal and private. Kept under wraps.

Confusion I feel. For loudly you speak of political persuasion. Assumptions made that others should listen. Loud-voiced. Disguised. Attempts at humor to undermine.

But what of your faith? Humble and precious. Should not your faith step forward in all directions? Not in lecture form. In the actions and spirit in which you live. Shouldn't God be more important than the next election?

I tell you for certain; it is not anyone's business my political direction.

But clear and hopeful as a sunset sky is my love and devotion.

ANGER SPILLING

Peaceful Passage

How saddened I am. Such beauty afforded to offer the world. Caught up you are in ego and hatred. Always blaming. Never truly grateful for life gifted. Never taking responsibility for actions delivered. Anger spilling against the rims of your existence.

Try reflection with courage. For it will take courage when reviewing the heartache you've inflicted. Feel the pain of your words and actions. Feel with the heart-place so carefully concealed. Covered with trophies and self-serving remedies. Covered beneath harsh-tongued relief.

Be the giver God intended. Not the executioner of character. For tearing down of others brings you lower to Earth Mother. Reach for the Heavens. Child of God. I've witnessed your beauty.

Compassion I gift. Praying for peaceful passage on this Earth journey. Reflect. Leave aside explanations. For in a world of genuine compassion, explanations are no longer needed.

DAWN OF A NEW DAY

Let Go

Today is the dawn of a new day. Let go of your burdens. Do not live in the past. Forgive yourself for things left undone. Learn from yesterday and try not to repeat the same life lesson. Rejoice in the wonders that envelope the moment. Challenge yourself to look for good and beauty in all—and in yourself.

Spend this day as though it was your last.

SEARCH WITH YOUR HEART

Homeless and Compassion

You passed a homeless person today.

Are you unsettled with the vision of the suffering of another soul or your lack of compassion? *Get a job,* you thought. *The burger shop is hiring.*

Tell me, have you gone without food? Have you gone without shelter? Have you gone without?

Before you answer, let me explain.

There are angels on Earth that walk among us. Not adorned with golden crowns or halos. They are in disguise. They are the humble, peaceful souls.

What if in passing a homeless person today, you looked with your heart instead of your ego. Would you feel their pain, their suffering? If you felt with your heart, instead of your ego—would you feel their Light?

We are all One. We are all Light. Search with your heart, not the ego.

CRUEL HOST DEMENTIA PLAYS
Peace and Patience

Inconvenienced and cross you've become. Heartfelt situation deprived of a solution. Recognize these emotions and then move on. Take of yourself inside and out. Prepare for the long haul.

Cruel host dementia plays. The mind wanders whilst the soul remains. Affection and prayers required. Soulful suffering now reigns for you and your dearest. Their uprooted passions and dreams remain unconcluded. Remembrances dissipated.

Worried you are for the price to you. Affecting your peace. Your serenity. Selfish worries, but understood.

In the coming days when teetering of tolerance reigns—may you be blessed with patience. Gift freely natural displays of love and tenderness. Their mind wanders—but the soul remains.

Peace, love, and serenity for you both.

RAINDROPS HALOED
Solid in Faith

Blessings for the smile you wear. Regardless the raindrops haloed over wetted hair. Solid in faith. Forever strong. Receiver and giver of God's love.

Blessings for the smile you wear. Open arms extended. Compassion delivered. From the heart-place where God is found.

Blessings, my friend. Seeker and keeper of faith. Through challenges, you stand firmly planted. Knowledge of God's promise. Life forever.

Blessings to you, my friend.

UNSTEADY TEETER

Spiritual Journey

You stand at the base of a spiritual journey. Two paths you unsteadily teeter. Exhausted. Unsure of direction. Weighing anger against peace.

My friend, the decision may be easily made. Close your eyes and follow the path of Light.

Child of God, you have been placed here for a reason. Your talents are desperately needed. Avoid the negative pulls of the planets and peoples. Actions and intentions should be for the greatest good of all, and not the appeasement of ego.

Travel in Light. Travel high. Highest of intentions in God's Light.

FAITHFUL LIFE

Judgment Free

Jumpy you are from one project to the next. Uncertainty your biggest enemy. Ambiguous direction. Stop for a moment. Inhale God's fresh air. Focus on the Light you carry within. Your talents are needed. Speak, preach, teach, and write to heal. Speak, preach, teach, and write to unite.

Giver of words and hope—learn to listen. Uncertainty is unnecessary—for uncertainty is absent in a faithful life. The world *is* topsy-turvy. Negativity threatens generations yet to come. Prayers and faith are crucial to even the keel.

Step it up a notch. Hold tight to the helm. You know what to do. When overwhelmed, portage yourself to calmer waters. Pray for peace and tranquility.

Giver of words and hope, trust your faithful intentions. Compassion and love are judgment-free.

PRAY FOR GUIDANCE
Uncertainties of Life

I have not the answer to life's uncertainness. Circumstances vary. Reasons sometimes untold. There are times when life is consumed with unsettledness.

Pray for guidance. Let God lighten the load. May you be gifted strength. Personal drive. May you progress through life's challenges with the greatest of ease. In harmony with nature, the Heavens, and earthly memories.

Personal dynamics and interactions come and go. No judgment. Compassion required. Lead by example. Strong in mind. Strong in body. For the greater benefit of your heavenly soul.

Pray for God's Light to see you through. The distance of headlights is all that is required.

SLICE OF A SENTENCE

Savor the Flavor

Writing. Speaking. Teaching. Preaching. Difficult it can be. Alone within. Working. Waiting. Hoping. My friend, the passage of the message is not the only intention. The passing of a message is the essence of you.

Driven you are to spew alphabetical arrangements like music to the sheet. Giving life to thought. Tedious. Yes. Plagued with peaks and fallows. It can be. But consumed you are with your pen. Consumed to put it out. Tending borrowed words until they find their place.

Dwell not on the process. Enjoy. Take a slice of a sentence and savor the flavor. True sometimes they fall from the sky. The wonderment of God's gift and glory.

Borrower of words . . . set free your imagination. Give life to your gift. Write. Speak. Teach. Preach.

WASTED TIME
Windows of Life

Wasted time. Watching, waiting, assuming. From the windows of your life. Calculating. Memorizing. Hoarder of details. Restless sleep preparing your case. If this—then take that. Hoping for discourse. Waiting and wishing to unload.

Wasted time. Stop watching. Turn away from your neighbors. At home, work, or play. Turn away from the situations that offer discourse. Turn away. Take a second. Take a breath.

For every bump or disruption, remember—we are of the same breath. Let go of the details haunting your rest. Let go of the hits behind the back. Let go of the watching, waiting, and assuming. Replace it with life.

Rage and internal unrest must be fed. Perseveration of facts. Replaying. Relaying. Angst to repay back.

End the torment.

Turn from your neighbors. Turn from the actions and disruptions of others. Turn to God's Light.

STRONG IN FAITH

Life's Gate

You run to the gate. Certain it opens to possibilities. Then hesitate. Surely it is the path for another. Fear of trespass overwhelms the thimble of dignity.

What is it you seek? What is your reason for being? For it is in this regard each person is unique.

You are here for a reason. Reflect. Your mission is much grander than you think. Sit with yourself. It will become clear. Look for the bigger picture.

An individual you are. Unique in the steps you take. Breathe in God's love. Stand tall. Stand strong in faith.

Open the gate.

Possibilities await.

ANGRY EDGE

Peace to Your Soul

Troubled I am for your angry edge. Hurt to your heart has set you off course. Bad remembrances and unrest. Pacing through life. Digesting and justifying rampaging indignations. A lifetime wasted on self-centeredness.

Set aside the hurt which has taken on a life of its own. Manifesting into hate and self-sabotaging performances. Save precious life energy and feed peace to your soul.

Recognize angry and misaligned intentions. Heal your distressed placement of affection. Find compassion for the imperfections of others. Then let the compassion flow to yourself.

Please, dear one, anger is an emotion that needs to be fed. Waste not one moment consumed with should-have-been. Let go of that which is harmful to you. Bring peace to your heart. Bring peace to your soul. Let go of the angry edge.

FORGIVENESS

Love from a Distance

Worry not. Hosted conversation I expected not. Difficult to speak pleasantly when actions and words have made the rounds amongst friends.

I've heard your ramblings—contagious meningitis of the mouth. 'Round and 'round conjectures twisted and turned, splashing against willing ears.

If ever to the batter's plate you wish to stand—I'll be waiting with heart in hand. Forgiveness granted. Offering peace to you through all God's graces.

Love you I do, but safely from a distance with my heart in tow. May God's blessings continue to shine. Take care. Be well.

GOD'S VOICE
Roar of a Wave

We are not alone.
God is always with us. His voice comes to us in many different ways.

From the cry of a baby to the roar of a wave. From a tear of hope to a warm embrace. It's carried by the wind from a homeless soul's lips to a rich man's fitful sleep.

God's voice runs through your veins.

HAPPINESS GIFTED
Seeker

Visible are the pangs across your brow. Unsettled and unhappy with the twisted turns of fate. Lost within. Sadness your closest friend.

My friend, look to your happiness as a possession to hold. You are the keeper. Maintainer. Guardian. If circumstances have bumped you off your feet, then change direction.

Look not to a job, person, object, or situation for that which you can only gift yourself.

Happiness.

Seek it. Keep it. Maintain it. Guard it. Happiness is the way in which you view your life.

EARTH DAY

Cascading the Globe

Tragic it is. So much waste. Waste of time. Waste of money. Waste of food. Waste of resources. Cascading the globe whilst empty bellies and strife is felt by the many. One person can make the difference. Change—positive in nature—is contagious to the whole. Shake free of the selfishness that keeps you idling on low.

Start small.

Empty your trash can of unnecessary debris. Compost. Recycle. Switch to natural and renewable energy.

Support organizations that feed. Support organizations that offer a bed and hot meal. Support organizations that work for the many—not the CEOs.

With ease the transition can be made when gifting to others. A cleaner planet. Children no longer left unfed.

We walk this journey together. Linked by our hearts and breath. We are of the same Father.

Look today not to what you need, but what can you do for another.

MISPLACED IDEALS

Grandness of Character

So much anger set in motion. The unforgiving blindness of the magnificence of others. Those devoted but deceived by misplaced ideals. Cascading wrath drifting across seas.

Beyond the harshness of life, the grandness of character exists. Goodness gifted. Energy spent for the betterment of this planet. Prayerful existence. Quietly spreading branches of a majestic tree of peace.

There will always be darkness harbored in the hearts of the sleeping, dreaming of glory through blitzing to pieces, peace-laden principles. Blocking the Light if we allow it.

Aware we need be of shadowed existence, but focused on the Light is of importance. Ground yourself in your beliefs. Hold hands with those of different nations and creed. Set your goals to be that of the highest. Future generations depend on it.

Focus on the Light. Join hands. Join hearts. Pray for everlasting peace. Pray for unity of nations.

LOVE GIFTED
Harm to None

Aware I am of the latest calamity. Worried for the troubled space in which you live. Love and comfort generously gifted. Sacred and precious. Suddenly displaced from your harmonious existence. The fault is not yours, but of the receiver of your devoted intentions. Their intentions of grandeur are at your expense; taking away more than just the dollar. A selfish and self-centered existence. Misguided gratitude returned in the form of malwishes.

    Forward you must tread. Carefully note those behaviors and tendencies so as not to gift away your heart and home *again*. Leave to the side the takers, liars, disruptors of life, stealers of sunsets, and good morning kisses. Send love and good wishes to them from a safe distance.

    Put energy into the golden Light you shine. Joyfully dance, create, read, pray, and write. Continue your life one with God. Love gifted to all and harm to none.

FORGOTTEN SENSATIONS
Wakeful Joy

The burden of life is heavy. Violence and strife continuously play on the big screen of our earthly journey. Radio, television, and the Internet upload negativity into wide-awake sleeping minds. Mundane routines play out like flat notes in a once sweet lullaby. The lullaby of life.

Where is the innocence of youth? Long ago forgotten memories of wakeful joy now replaced with dread and sorrow. Dread for what is and dread for what is to come. Sorrow for what is and sorrow for what was.

The burden of life can be heavy if you look at the whole.

Find the child-like excitement for play, exploration, forgotten lullabies, and the subtle songs of nature. Awake the child within. Anxious to play. Anxious with expectations for moments of happiness.

Hold onto the child-like expectation of the moment to see you through the whole.

GOD'S GIFT
Second Chances

No words of sympathy, my friend. The mud you wallow in is of your own demise. Spewing a campaign to maim and brutalize. Look to another for an open ear. Closed is mine.

Stop in this place of circling karma. Stop. Plant your feet in another direction.

God has gifted a life of second chances. Chances to make a change. In a moment. Without notice. Change.

But the decision must be that of your own. Leave your soiled shoes at the door. Step into a life carpeted with Light. Happiness. A peaceful existence.

What was—was. This is now.

No words of sympathy, my friend. Words of encouragement with a message of hope.

TROUBLING TIME

Embrace Light

It is a troubling time. Anger revs to the brim of societies. Invoked and provoked by power-hungry individuals for political gains. Fingers pointed. Arms raised. Joyfully, the media rushes to deliver.

My friend, awareness of the state of things need not mean embracing the negativity. Do not give it power.

Embrace the positive. Remember the love once felt for a brother—before you knew how he voted. Remember the compassion once felt for a person of a different origin—before you learned to fear. Remember the prayers of your youth—before you thought you were the center of the universe.

My friend, it is as easy as breathing. Look through the shadows. There is Light. Do not give power to negative influences. Give power to God's Light.

For every hurtful act against man and planet, offer prayer. For every hurtful act, there is hope. You will see it, too. Simply look through the shadows to the Light.

UNIVERSAL SUFFERING

Let God

Your suffering goes not unnoticed. Momentous rampage across the valley of your life. Universal in form. Unique in detail. Comradery shared of a sorrowful sort.

You're convinced enough time has passed. You sit expressively exhausted, craving the simplest of life's harmony. Sure the last tear has shed. But disheartenment follows another tearful flow. Alone within. For although suffering is universal, individuals we become when grief comes to call.

Let God carry the burden so great. Shout to the Universe for peace from bereavement. Peace from death's shadow choking life's happiness. Peace to your heart. Peace to your soul.

A loved one lost may never be replaced. But peace from the pain will come through God's grace.

HEAVENLY DESIGN

Your Calling

Worry I do for your stop-watched existence. Minutes rationed by another's intentions. Quickly life passes. Precious energy wasted on the sidelines of life. Losing sight of your goals and personal achievements. Clapping and encouraging a false reality.

Every person has a predestined mission. Unique and vital to the good of the whole. Stop watching. Start living. Follow *your* calling. Your talents are most needed. The world is upside down.

Courage it takes to make the change. Gifted you are with all that is needed. Worry not, my friend. The journey is exciting; pleasure you'll take in your *own* achievements.

Listen to the small voice inside. Intuition. Subconscious. Your definition of choice. Follow the path heavenly designed.

I'll be clapping and encouraging as I follow mine.

ASSUMPTIONS AND JUDGEMENTS

Shoes of Another

You carry a peculiar sense of your place in this world. Anger and arbitration in the forefront. Hastily delivering statements and actions justified by assumptions and judgments. Powerful and smug. Anger is the center of your universe. Not mine.

Ask of yourself. What is your intention? Puffing and beating of the chest make this not a better place. Let go of assumptions and judgments. You have not tripped and fallen in the shoes of another. Dispense with the tongue. Lend a hand.

Child of God, your brethren are your brothers and sisters. Regardless of their place. Preference might be for uplifting actions. Compassionately speaking. Compassionately driven.

Puff and beat your chest. Beat your heart with the love of humanity. Take in a deep, fresh breath of God's grace. Your essence is compassion.

Change the center of the universe from yourself to someone else.

DAYS TALLY
Walk with God

Understand I do. Days tally. Ancient rhythm painted across a furrowed face. Wisdom and love reckoned and dismissed. Within you sit. Alone with thought. One thing to remember. Alone you are not. For God forever sits within your heart. Each step and breath is taken with His grace.

Hold His love. Reflect His compassion. Good deeds to be done until the end of your path. Change focus, my friend. A voice of wisdom and love need never be dismissed. Change of audience, perhaps. Share your patinaed grasp of life. It is a gift. Walk proudly with God until your last step.

Your voice is sorely needed.

FORGIVENESS KNOT
Live Life Forward

It's so much easier than you think. Options are varying to different degrees. The weight you carry needlessly. Tied and shackled to the past. Waste of energy. Let go. Release.

Unsettling distractions drawn together with outstretched palms. Tenderly wrapped in satin lace. Majestically tied and sealed. A forgiveness knot so sacredly placed.

Forgiveness granted is sacred indeed. To others. Especially yourself. Mistakes happen. Choices sometimes better made. The weight you carry is of the should-have-been. To live life forward, you must let go of the past. Keep lessons learned. Forgiveness granted for the rest.

Sit within yourself. Search the hurts and misplaced intentions and one-by-one address. Recognize and give gratitude for the place held within your past. Pull tight upon the forgiveness knot. Then ever so gently . . . release. Feel the weight drift away. Making space for love and compassion. For yourself and perhaps someone else.

Let go of the past. It's *the now* that reigns. Make room in your heart-place for love and compassion.

STILLNESS OF YOU

Intentions Heard

Exhaustion spills across your sweated brow. Blank-marble gazes from eyes once ignited. What earthly race do you run? You're tired. Aspirations to get ahead, but you fall behind in the pleasures of life.

Can you stand quietly in the stillness of you? Look to the Heavens with gratitude. Quiet the self-inflicted commotion. Listen intently to heart tugs of sincerity and forgotten moments of inspiration. There's strength to move mountains with mere intentions.

Courage it takes to reach for heavenly goals. Betterment of the whole without monetary reward. Would not a race be better won when the prize is gifted to another?

Reignite the flame. Run a different race. Feed the homeless. Shake a stranger's hand. Smile at everyone when out-and-about. Hum softly. Pray for those less fortunate. Pray for humility. Pray for humanity. Plant flowers.

Uplifting and positive actions gifted to the human race. These are the defining moments when life's journey ends and the race is won.

GIFTED ANOTHER DAY
Give Gratitude

I've been there. Mornings wasted swathed in man-made prints against cotton ribbing. Shielding the Light. Exhaustion follows a restless night.

Dear one. My dear one. Pull the draping of burdens from your face. Listen as trumpets of geese welcome God's pink-palette sky.

Leave at your feet the nightgown of earthly trepidations. Ego, challenges, and self-inflicted limitations. Go forth this day like no other. Go forth burden free.

A good morning kiss God has gifted. Waste not one moment covering your face. He'll manage your burdens. He will pave the way. Open your heart to miracles. Push away the bed-linen blinds. Give gratitude for the sunrise. Give gratitude for billowy designs against God's lush sky.

Today is a good day to be alive. Face the day with gratitude and grace.

TOXIC RELATIONSHIP
Gate Locked and Sealed

Mistaken you are for my outward façade. Withholding of love you are mistaken. Simply, enough said. Conversations delinquent.

An unhealthy and toxic path this relationship has taken. Passage of time in my personal space you are forbidden. Gate now locked and sealed. In my heart, you shall always remain. Love unswayed. Be well, my friend, but far from my personal space.

May God grace you abundance of peace, joy, and new relationships.

SHIELD OF LAUGHTER
Realize Your Worthiness

I see you shielded behind the laughter. Witty and fun-loving to the masses.

I see you masked in sadness. Filling your heart with the laughter of others instead of your own.

Look within detached from humor. Look with the compassion shown others. Sit for a while with yourself. Realize your worthiness.

You are a person full of compassion, kindhearted, and intelligent. Let go of the hidden sadness. Relearn to laugh in a heartfelt way. Laugh until your stomach jiggles and tears run freely down your face. Then wipe away the tears of happiness. Clear vision remaining of the person I see. A child of God. Radiant in Light.

Realize your worthiness in God's eyes. Witty and fun loving you still can be. Genuine in laughter truly your own.

LET YOUR LIGHT SHINE

Worthy a Beautiful Life

Sunshine filled days I wish for you. In your home and when about. Ache does my heart for the path you have chosen. Locked within. Everything kept out. Shielded from prying eyes and questions. Sequestered in darkness. Barricaded windows blocking life. Maneuvering amongst stacked and piled remnants of a once productive life. Tripping over scattered and tossed debris.

The problem perhaps is the perception of self. You are worthy of more. You are worthy a beautiful life. Open the windows of your heart. Let in the Light! Beauty abounds. Beginning with you. A gentler and kinder soul there never could be. Hide not from the life God has so generously gifted. Clean out the debris that blocks your Light.

Dust the mirror. Take another look. A robust child still lives within. Hide not from society. Hide not from yourself. You are the best of the best. So much to offer. So much to give.

Open the windows. Open your heart. Blessed you are. Don the sunglasses. Let God's Light within and about.

LONELINESS

Strands of a Web

I hear what you say. Passionate voice. Words clearly spoken. Alone you believe for most of your life. Consoling with self-pity and angry disbelief. Unworthy of notice and companionship. I hear what you say. Different opinion have I. Alone you have never been.

Travel this journey abandoned we do not. Our paths are woven like the strands of a web. Each strand glistens on its own in the Light. Hologram designs fashioned of intersecting lives.

An individual you are, that is true. Alone you will never be. Connected to this planet and all that it holds. God's Light. You. Me. Mountains. Forests. Waterways. Farmers' fields. Honey bees. Lands and people far away. Commonalities and connections shared.

Attitude and vision are all that is required. See the life God has gifted. Welcome warm smiles and peaceful interactions. Reciprocate. Acknowledge the hologram designs and connections.

Take the strand of your life. Weave a new web. Long and happy with many intersecting threads.

LIFE GIFTED

Nature's Toll

I laugh at our antics. Humor the best discourse for nature's toll. The mind remains strong whilst the hands become feeble. Hair whitens. The body ages like yellowed photographs taken a time long ago.

Honor the life gifted. Honor each breath. Find humor in the changes that happen. Look to the positives. Aging is a natural process. Bottoms and breasts sag, for men and women alike. And, then there's—forgetfulness. But also comes the gift of compassion and an understanding of the universe through vetted life experiences.

Closer to God. Closer to nature. Closer to children. Closer to those that go without. Closer to answering the questions youth pivots around.

Aging is a blessing. A gift from God. Laugh through the changes.

The best is yet to come.

VERSES SONGS PAINTINGS
Spread Goodwill

I commend your diligence. Sequestered from society. Your gifts break cycle. Phrasings, songs, and paintings gather momentum. Releasing caged knowledge.

Your energy rises. Gifted talents from above. Time is short. You were late for roll call.

Words, songs, and images setting the foundation for the union of hearts. Significant in this place and time lacking goodwill and compassion. A reminder is needed. We are all one.

Alone you sit penning philosophies. Bellowing heartfelt melodies. Slathering paint across paper. Spreading contagious intentions of benevolence. A virus worth catching. Much depends on the weight you carry.

Catch up you must. Remember . . . you were late for roll call. Confirm higher intentions with action. Verses set to paper. Songs sung loudly. Paintings brightly crafted.

UNSETTLED WITHIN
God's Embrace

Lost you seem. Unsettled in yourself. Behavior like a crying child, inconsolable. My friend, sometimes the child within seeks attention.

Please know you need not go far. For by your side God awaits. Gift to God your unsettledness. Feel his embrace. Weep you will in the magnitude of His grace.

Stretch with your heart. In this moment of time. Regardless of location. Feel the surge of joy and compassion. Shed your loneliness.

My wish for you, dear one, is happiness.

STRENGTH OF HUMANITY
Diversity in Light

The strength of humanity rests not on the shoulders of one representative of political or religious persuasion. The strength of humanity is built on the Light that laces the strands of diversity into one. The blending of talents, knowledge, religions, beliefs, struggles, loves, and compassion.

The strength of humanity is in the unity of the whole as a whole. Honoring our differences. Understanding our unified connection to the planet.

The strength of humanity rests on the shoulders of all. Responsibility taken, not tacked onto another. Through our power as individuals, we strengthen the whole.

Stand strong. Stand tall. Stand for values and intentions of the highest calling. Be the voice that whispers others from the darkness. Be the hands that feed the hungry. Be the heart sharing compassion. Be the feet that walk straight toward the Light leading others.

Unity of the whole as a whole. That is the strength of humanity.

SPIRITUAL LADDER
Upward Looking

I've been in your place more times than I'd like to remember. Struggling with humanness. Striving to do better. Sloppily slipping backward from time to time.

Easy it is not when perseverating on past tenses. What was done. Who said what. Actions taken. Emotions inflated.

Another option there might be. Forward momentum. Upward direction. Inward reflection.

Struggling with humanness is a continuous dilemma. Ease the transition upward by looking inward. Acknowledge your part in any given situation. Reflect. Learn.

Climb one more rung up the spiritual ladder.

HEART STILL BROKEN

Delicacy of Life

Gratitude is difficult to find when your heart is broken. The loss you suffer can never be replaced. Today, my friend, take baby steps out of yourself. Out of your grief. Walk through nature. When gratitude seems insurmountable—*start small*.

Look to the wonders God has placed beneath your feet. Lightly tread. Soft grass. Wildflowers. Clover. Weeds. Each is struggling to survive. Like you. Give gratitude. Give gratitude for pebbles and sea-worn glass. Give gratitude for waves crackling against a familiar reef or rocky cliff ledge.

After you see the beauty that still exists, easier it will be to see on a grander scale. Memories gently tucked and folded. Awaiting your embrace when ready, my friend.

Until then, tread lightly upon this Earth place. Damage not the smallest of wonders God has placed. Reminders of the delicacy of life, loved ones, and times better spent.

ANGER VULNERABILITY SORROW

Step into God's Light

Into the depths of emotion you travel, leaving behind a trail of shattered glass. Arm's length distancing your heart from others. Renouncing humanity. Renouncing faith.

My friend, it is time to let go. Beautiful child of God, sometimes dreams shatter. Trails harbor bumps. Broken hearts happen. Relationships fall apart. It is called *life*.

Let go of the rampaging emotions. Anger. Vulnerability. Sorrow. Take back your power. Take control of your life. Forge a new path. Firm footing awaits. Grab hold of God's hand. Walk together and travel untethered of the emotional weight.

Live life. Love life. Open your heart to others. Connect with humanity. Connect with God. Step into God's Light and step into yourself.

HONOR LIFE GIFTED

Heavenly Connection

I am not sure which is worse. Ignorance of suffering or apathy of life. You think you're awake. You are not. Dreaming behind a sleeping reality. Siren sounding. Time to wake up!

Look about. Suffering, hunger, sadness, isolation, hatred, and earthly devastation.

Take notice. Take action.

Join me uniting the nations in prayer. One small voice can make a difference. Honor your life. Your talents are needed. Smiles, handshakes, joyful interactions. Wake to what God has gifted. A mind to think. Hands to take action. A soul heavenly connected. Honor your talents and blessings.

Impossible you say, to reach the masses.

Stand corrected my friend. Kindled deeds of good actions *will* combust, lighting the spark and the way for another. You and me first. Let's get started.

Waste not one moment. Help is needed. Awake and take part in the compassionate surge for humanity.

BELIEVE

Shadow Cast

You exist in the shadow cast from another instead of basking in that of your own. Step forward from self-doubt. You were put here for a reason. Limitless are your possibilities for growth. Believe in your talents. Believe that one person can make a difference.

Your heart. Your intentions. Your goodness. The essence of you *is* contagious.

Step forward from the shadow. Make your presence known. Run with the life so preciously gifted.

Make your existence count.

LIFE ETERNAL
Promised by God

It is nothing to be reckoned with. It knows us by name. We all get the call. Fear not the thought of loss of breath, for life is eternal. Promised by God.

No guarantees for length or breadth of this path traveled. Wring the most from each day. Smile sweeter. Love deeper. Laugh harder. Forgive faster. Shine brighter. Speak from your heart. Live your faith. Trust in the promise God has made. Life is eternal.

United again we all shall be.

TORMENTED EXISTENCE

Courage to Stand Tall

Courage it takes. Courage to stand tall in the awareness of you. Awareness of unfortunate choices and bonds made with intersecting personalities. New direction now followed. No longer told what to do. What to say. How to act. Where to go. What to wear. No longer squashed beneath a toe-plated boot. You know who you are. Strong. Courageous. Beautiful. Child of God.

Ignorant are those tormenting your existence with hurtful dialogue. Swollen egos cradled on the demise and undoing of innocence. The expanse of time devoted to hate-ridden slander. Ambitious in self-glorification.

Courage it takes to stand against and let go. Send forward prayers of gratitude for separation from the foul coarseness. Safely tucked away in a world your own. You have reflected. You have found *you*. Confident and controlled. Peaceful and genuine on the path now so carefully chosen.

Child of God. Always there will be dark-sided ignorance. Follow the grace and Light God has provided.

ACTIONS OF ONE

God's Breath

There is no beginning, and there is no end. Energy to energy in one form to another. Created to be compassionately virtued. Adorned in God's Light. Shining in goodness. Decisions based on the benefit of the whole.

One moment taken whilst your head still rests upon morning's first light. One moment to be thankful for this day gifted. Pray for guidance. That each step and word to be carefully taken. Herding and guiding through positive example.

There is no beginning, and there is no end. From God's breath you were created. Child of God. Pray for guidance. Forget not the important role you play. May your direction be of the highest intention.

CLOVER TO BUTTERCUPS
High Expectations

Let not one day pass without high expectations. Expectations that moments of wonder, excitement, and pleasure will fill your day. Then, give thanks.

Spread your wings as a tender butterfly on its virgin flight. Look and see what is before your eyes. Pigeons and songbirds that litter city fences and rooftops majestically coo. Clover and buttercups burst from the soil in contrasting colors along sidewalks and farmers' fields alike. Children, different as buttercups and clover, spread God's Light in innocent and glorious play.

Warm smiles, well wishes, and embraces from forged friendships are not the necessities of life, but as a communal existence. We are all the same breath.

Waste not one moment. Look for the beauty. Look for what is wonderful, exciting, and pleasurable in all that you do, in all of your travels, and with all of God's creations.

We are all the same breath. From pigeons to songbirds, clover to buttercups, to the children of many colors and to the different songs they sing. There is such beauty in this life.

SHOES OF ANOTHER
Spiritual Ladder

Fear-driven you are and unable to stand on your own. Caught up in the anger and ego of another. Their mission accomplished. Translated to your agenda. Quick to quip. Quick to knife. Mob mentality and personal war. Maiming innocents and creating unnecessary strife. Cowardly attacks from the sidelines of life.

Your journey was meant to be your own.

You assist in the ruckus instead of minding your business. You're in where you don't belong. Step away from gang-like chatter. Humbly walk in the shoes of another. Feel the stony path beneath their feet. Do you have the courage to see what they've handled? To rally their life challenges and feel their grief?

Humble yourself. Then stand tall. You'll have passed another life lesson. One more rung up the spiritual ladder.

SOCIETY'S NEGLECT
Heaven's Light

Wooden floor. Dusty and cold. Shoveled into cracks. Hidden from sight. Inexcusable neglect.

Woven tapestry of tangled locks. Precious child lacking sustenance and love. Evidence of a once heavenly soul.

Abandoned rocking chair. Her sole embrace. Whilst lifeless arms drape. No one there to console.

Gone is the strength to lift the fragile head.

Heaven's Light.

Society's disgrace.

Matters not the location. Home or abroad. Suffering child. Society's neglect.

TODAY IS FOR LIVING

Teapot Screams

There you sit as the teapot screams for release from the heat. Consumed with a handful of yellowed photographs sprawled across a scratched and dusty table. These are the memories you keep. *Once again* and *if only*. The cornucopia of the past.

What sits in your horn of plenty? Plenty of happiness? Or sorrow? Plenty of love? Or loneliness? Plenty of memories? Or fear of tomorrows?

The past was. The now is. The tomorrows will come. Today is for living. Regardless the contents in your horn of plenty.

Look not to what life *has* offered, but to what life *can* offer. Look not to what was, and expect nothingness in your tomorrows. Fill your horn of plenty with dreams fulfilled. Sit not with your photographs whilst the teapot sputters.

Pull back the threadbare drapes. Allow in God's Light. Open the window to a fresh spring breeze. Let the photographs blow from the table. Dust off the past. Seek the blessings of this moment.

So often you forget. You are in charge of today. Whether you grieve or fear for hurts hurdled. You are responsible for your happiness. Even a broken teacup from a matched set has purpose. Find your place in this moment of time. Worry not, for your horn of plenty will fill itself when you live each day to the fullest.

Go now to the window of life. Take this gifted day and all others. Give gratitude. Release the screeching teapot from the heat.

WEIGHT OF THE WORLD
Butterfly Graces

The weight of the world you carry upon your back. Of family. Of things undone. Of fears hauled from the past. Of hopes slipping away. Successes just short of fingertips callused and worn. What holds you back?

Look to your ankles shackled with doubt. Doubts about your worthiness. Doubts about your abilities and talents. Doubts more than I can count. My friend, the restraints are in your head. One step forward is all that is needed. One step forward on this journey of life. Have faith in your abilities and your connection to God.

More worthy you could not be. Child of God. Beautiful in your heart. Beautiful in your intentions. You are here for a reason.

Set free your butterfly graces. Set free the amazing person I know you to be. Set free the power within. Fly butterfly. Be all that you can be.

A MIRACLE BESTOWED

Depths of Sadness

Fear is the equalizer.
Fear of the unknown. Fear of the unfamiliar. Fear of solitude. Fear of loss.

You entered your loft, drapes drawn and lights out. You sat in darkness.

From the depths of sadness, the Universe embraced you offering comfort within the rocking of Earth's motion. Morning to night, morning to night, morning to night.

You sat alone. Wondering why the world, God, and all souls had forsaken you. Friends loved deeply, turned and disappeared without the slightest trace, leaving shadows of mere memories haunting your daily existence. You cried.

Did you not love enough?

You begged to return to the arms of your Creator. And then. . . .

Giving yourself to the Universe, you asked to be healed. Expected to be healed. With your head planted upon the bosom of Earth Mother, you grounded yourself within Her strength and everlasting love and beauty; awakening to the unfolding of your soul. Your inner strength began to emerge.

A miracle was bestowed upon you. God ushered you through the darkness to peace and tranquility. Love cascading in a blanket of heavenly Light, lifting the sadness.

Peace replaced sorrow. Knowing replaced ignorance. Love and forgiveness filled the empty caverns of your heart.

You are one with God.

PATH TAKEN

Heavenly Direction

Different choices you could have made. Judge and jury . . . not my place.

In the future, just remember, you have free choice. If heading on a crooked path, watch for the detour of Light to bring you back.

Follow your faith. God is Lighting the way.

LIFE LIVED FULL
Laughter Heard

Sorry I am for those left behind. For yours was a life lived fully. Playful laughter. Devotion to family. Love of friends. Intensity of emotions. A heart bigger than life. Laughter still heard through generations' heartfelt embrace.

Offer words of sympathy for you I cannot. For you now walk with God. Carrying a warrior's shield in God's army, filling the void you've left with Light. Reminding family and friends the importance of now. Awareness instead of ignorance. Do the best. Be the best. Love the most. Laugh the loudest. Play the hardest.

You are missed.

MOTHER'S DAY

Share Bread

If only there were glasses that conveyed vision through the eyes of a mother.

Through the eyes of a mother, neighbors would love neighbors and forgiveness would be extended.

Through the eyes of a mother, potential would be praised. For the focus of a mother's vision is what's there, not what's missing.

Through the eyes of a mother, God's Light would be obvious. For a mother sees the spark that others fail to see.

If only there were glasses that gave vision through the eyes of a mother. Compassion would displace anger, and there would be no enemies.

If you looked to your neighbor, co-worker or stranger on the street with the vision of mother, how then would you view those in need? A homeless person left to the streets. A child without food. A person in need. Through the eyes of a mother, heartbreaking indeed.

Look through the eyes of a mother. We are of the same breath. Love all with compassion and create a world where children are fed, and the homeless have a place to sleep. A world without enemies. Come, sit at my table. I will share bread.

TEETERING DIRECTION

Pray

Teetering you are, caught between the signs of life. The mind demanding one way and the heart gently directing to another. Struggle no more. When in doubt, simply pray.

Every person has a gift. The ability to reason. The ability to listen. Think it you, God, or Holy Spirit. Matters not. Directional signs are gifted. Live your life in a joyful manner. Soar, my friend, to the mountaintops. Lift your spirit high. Your words and actions transcend miles. Touching the heart of others. Touching mine.

Allow for clarity of prayer. Ask your questions, and then listen. Still in doubt? Simply *listen*.

ROUGH SPOTS TRAVELED
Patience and Love

I hold you in my heart as to your tiny hand I once clung. The rough spots you travel require patience and love. Strength and courage are not enough. For the battle you fight is in your heart.

A life path thwarted with sadness, pain, and frustration is a blessing in disguise. Those are mere storms before seeing Light.

God has gifted options for a life full. Peaceful interactions. Stress removed.

Follow the Light. A clear path to God has been provided. Patience, my friend. Open your heart to God's love and grace.

SHADOWS BENEATH FAMILIAR FACES
White Doves

I understand your heartfelt pangs. Perplexing it is. When first seeing an old friend in a new light. Eyes darkened. Heart cold as night. Tongue forked. Wearing the actions two-faced times seven. Shivers sent to your spine. Give gratitude for awareness of the shadows beneath faces familiar. You did right. Nothing offered. Nothing to be taken.

Pray for your friend. Compassion for the bumpy path that awaits. For all deeds, good and bad, have a way of finding their way back. Send white doves to fill their empty heart-place. Keep your distance. Remain gracious.

Allow in your private circle those that walk in Light.

WASTE NOT
Follow God's Light

Waste not one moment. There's much to be done! Stories to be told. Pictures to be painted. Songs to be sung. Never take for granted time on this walk.

The choice is yours. Skip happily or trip grudgingly over life's pleasantries. The vision of tranquility or cradling bad memories. Two paths beneath your feet. One straight with ease. Sweet fragrances of nature and fresh air. Blindingly bright. The other crooked and steep. Fouled with remembrances dark and deep. Look. It is plain to see. For what you search for will run underneath.

Follow God's Light. Savor the journey. This earth walk is easier than you think.

BATTLE THE PAGE

Let Your Words Bloom

Struggle you do. Unnecessarily so. Battling blankness. Straining to pluck sentences from the air. Rereading and rephrasing. My friend, perfection is not the goal. Worry not for proper diction. Gaps and holes will fill in later. Just let go.

Let your words bloom like desert flowers across the barren page. Words gifted to you. Not to hold or barter. Borrower of words, share your verses so carefully tended. Decorate the paper with delicate blooms. Don't resist. Relax. Revise. Then let go.

The process *is* a challenge, but the words are free. Speaker, teacher, writer, and preacher—gift to the world your tended verses.

WEIGHTED EXISTENCE

Cleanse

Heavily you wear your weighted existence. So much stuff. Hoarder you've become. Holding, storing, stacking. Avoiding at all cost. Afraid to let go. My friend, peace will follow a good cleaning out.

Clean out your cupboards. Clean out your heart. Discard, give back, or donate. Let go of bad memories and angst. Cluttered life, home, and heart.

Let go of that which no longer serves. Gift it to someone else. Cleanse with patience. Cleanse with love.

Walk lightly in this time and space. Keep what is needed. Let go of the rest. Make room for new memories and experiences.

This life is gifted. Give back.

CROOKED CHOICES
Better Tomorrow

Feverish dreams plague your sleep. All the *what-ifs* in a repetitive saga. Dear one, let go. Let go of what no longer *is*. The past is over. The future remains. Courage and hope in the moment-to-moment will make the difference. Give gratitude. For what lessons would there be in a life complacent? Perhaps of benefit are the lessons of love and patience. Hope and faith. Sometimes restlessness sprouts the seeds for change. Change from yesterday's crooked choices to strength for straighter tomorrows.

When you lay upon your bed visualize hope, happiness, peace, and compassion. Invite God to hear your prayers. Open your heart to His love and compassion. Believe in yourself. You were put here for a reason. You are needed.

Wipe your sweat-laden brow. Fluff and realign within.

May peace reign through your dreams and along straightened choices.

ATTENTION-GETTING BEHAVIOR
Good of the Whole

I see your pranks. Attention-getting behavior. Showboat performance at the expense of others. Unaware you are of your own intention. My friend, better to be remembered for acts of kindness, generosity, humility, and compassion. Turn that energy into something grand. Larger than your human self. Turn that energy into releasing God's Light.

A place upon this Earth you have. Important in the scheme of things. Use your energies for the whole of humanity. Spreading laughter is an important role. Spread it with the highest of intentions. Spread it for the greater good of all.

Release your Light. Grandstand for the greater good of the whole.

GRACE

Smallest of Shoes

Each step gingerly placed. Heel to toe. Heel to toe. Forward on. This planet you grace.

You have a place. You have a reason. You are needed, regardless of past steps taken.

Take the time to recognize your footprint upon this place.

Forward momentum.

Sometimes, it is the smallest of shoes that carry the most weight.

SHELTERING THE BLOWS

Light against Shore

I wish to wrap my heart around you, sheltering the blows. Aware I am of the gravity of the situation. Round-shouldered. Defeated. Dragging from one moment to the next. Sadness overwhelms as *what is* crumbles to the ground. Your view narrowed and skewed.

If only.

If only you could see the Light against the shore offering strength for direction and hope for a better tomorrow.

The *what if* and *if only* are in the past. Life beats and challenges, forcing the same path. Resist temptations to stay put. Look to the Light. Follow with your heart a *safer* direction. Peace, love, and compassion await. Sometimes the brightest Light follows the greatest storm.

Go. Find your way. Closely carry God, your faith, and my heart.

BATTLES FOUGHT
Peace Deprived

Returned you have from the ravages of war. Great battles won, but the fight remains. Struggling with memories and depression. Matters not that the war is done when the internal battle continues. Invisible demons robbing precious moments of joy. Sleep deprived. Peace deprived, even at home.

You're going through the motions. Award-winning actor, or so you think. Convinced loved ones see not the Ying and Yang of your personality shifts. My friend, they know. They suffer for you. Oblivious to your challenges, they are not.

Pray for a miracle. Release the memories that replay against the inner walls of your mind. Ask for a quieting and a release from the war-induced demons that *do* affect your home and life. Seek refuge in God's Light. Pray for a miracle. You are not alone. *God stands by your side.*

TRAFFIC OF LIFE
Blessings to You

Easy to become caught in the traffic of life. Blinded by the gifts and beauty of each moment. These are my wishes for you on this God-gifted day.

May you learn to trust. Trust in yourself. Trust in God.

May you find faith. Faith in yourself. Faith in God.

May you learn to be happy. Happy with yourself. Happy in God's love.

May you accept praise. Praise yourself for good deeds done. Praise for God's love.

May you learn to see. See the beauty you carry within. See the beauty of God that abounds.

May you be humble and grateful. Grateful for all your blessings. Grateful to God for all life's lessons. Humble in God's love.

Blessings to you, my friend. Look to the beauty within and the beauty about. Take a breath. Feel God's love.

MEASURE OF WORTH

Preacher Teacher Speaker Writer

I read the tiredness in your eyes. You've traveled a distance in such a short while. Waned from society. Skills honed and then tweeted. Hoping for a break. Time is ticking. You started late.

Preacher, teacher, speaker, writer. So many hats generate. Pressure from the sidelines urges you back into place. Pointed fingers. Laughter behind your back. You stagger from the path. Seconding guessing with a mirrored eye the sidelines' chatter. After all, maybe they're right. After all, preacher, teacher, speaker, writer—those are the positions for persons of caliper. They're the studied, educated, intellectual, and cultivated.

You ask God, "What path am I to take?"

God takes your hands. Tugging gently at first. Reminding you to preach, teach, speak, and write from the heart-place. For you are the studied of life. The educated in compassion. The intellectual thinker that puts thoughts into action. You are the cultivated amongst angels. You are the preacher, teacher, speaker and writer. You are the qualified for you are awake. What better person to deliver from the heart? What better person to whisper God's message?

Harbor not a confusion of caliper. Only God is worthy of measuring your worth.

One foot in front of the other. Stay to your path. Preacher. Teacher. Speaker. Writer.

GRIEF

God's Light

Mournful cries adorn the darkened moments of an otherwise bright life. Your grief is your own. Carried close to your heart. You dictate the manner in which you weep. You dictate the time required.

Sufferer of heartache . . . you are not alone. God follows along reminding you of the promise made, for after this life comes another. United in Heaven you shall be when time dictates.

Make the best of the journey remaining. You were left behind for a reason. Look for the beauty and peace that exists. Pain in your heart you will always carry. But easier it will be when aware of God's glory.

Find the reflection of loved ones lost in the beauty that surrounds the moment. Early morning dew twinkling on clover. A sunset memory tenderly concealed.

Shed your tears of heartache. It is your right. But lose not sight of God's Light.

FRAILTY OF HEART
Laborer of God

Sadly you focus on the perception of self. Alone on a mission. Frailty of heart. Lost in the shuffle, or so you believe. Fearful and shy, but a giant in my eyes.

My friend, your heart is so grand. It enters the room before you. Expanding through the blanketed darkness. Shining ever so brightly. You are a laborer of God. Linking suffering souls to faith and hope. Retying spiritual connections severed and worn. Your placid energy is needed. The space you fill overflows with love. Embracing and greeting. Gentle smile. Gentle soul.

FRIENDSHIP EMBRACED

Purity of Love

Blessed I am for the tightly-worn cloak of friendship embraced. Matters not the passage of time or distant location. Two voices familiar. Two hearts entwined. Bonded through shared experiences.

Gratitude given. For through the ups and downs of crooked trails taken, by my side you remain. Judgement cast away. Compassionately embraced.

Wonder I do, to what chance I should have a friend such as you. Blessed I am. Blessed.

RAVAGING CELLS
Prayers to You

So sorry to hear of your newest challenge. Ravaging cells stealing happiness. Threatening life. You are not alone through the unexpected turns of late. Light exists beyond the shadowed night. Look to your faith. Find strength.

Prayers to you, dear one. Comfort you will find through faith.

GLORY OF GOD

Joining of Hearts

A call to action. The time is now. Brothers and sisters of all nations and religions. Brothers and sisters uniquely different yet bound together through journey and breath. Join hearts and hands in the prayerful union and God's grace.

Look to your brethren with a heart that is open. Recognize the glory of God carried within. Matters not a person's status, color, or place of worship. What matters is the joining of prayer and kindhearted actions.

What is the reason for being? Acquisitions matter little when the heart grows cold. Give of yourself. Give to another. Give of your time. Give of your prayerful intentions for the benefit of all.

AWAKENING
Forgiveness Relieved

Awakening to the Light of day—an emotional process. Reflection on indiscretions. Transgressions. Sorrowful interactions. Past the painful awareness, you will go to a peaceful place. Forgiveness relieved.

Understanding comes when walking in Light. The place you serve. The importance of one. Actions and intentions most peaceful and kind. Passed off unknowingly. Lifting those distressed. Lifting those seeking. Those hurting. Those still angry and at unrest.

Finish the process. Cry tears of release, relief, and gratitude. Awake to the peace and joy of walking in God's Light.

Blessings to you, my friend.

RAGING ANGER
Fear Manifested

There is something I have come to learn. Fear can manifest as raging anger. Reckless actions crushing innocents of passive behavior. When fear takes hold, it runs the show. Strength within required to recognize the difference—a life of peace or life strained and alone.

Recognize with compassion *their* fear realized. Fear of abandonment. Fear of embarrassment. Fear of discovery. Fear of insignificance in the Universe. Fear of simply the unknown. Unknown beliefs, habits, or origins of another soul.

Let not the darkness of *their* rage and ignorance fall upon you. Protect yourself and your heart. Tolerate nothing that damages your person or soul.

GOD'S GIFTED BREATH

Reconciliation

Years unravel. A once magical relationship sacrificed. Can you remember what you're mad about? Waging war for what reason? Petty differences? Exposing and toting anger for another? Jealousy? Hurt feelings? Blimps on the ego?

Tell me, what holds you at arm's length? This distance created for pain.

If you had but one chance to reconcile . . . would you grasp so tightly to the entity you have created . . . or would you let go?

No guarantees on this Earth walk. Is anger worth the sacrifice to your soul?

Today God has gifted breath. Be grateful. Open your heart to love. Open your heart to reconciliation. Open your heart to forgiveness.

Pick up the phone. Make that call.

SING THROUGH WORDS

Rainbow Colored Pages

Which hat is it you wear today? Parent. Teacher. Friend. Writer. Speaker. Preacher. Pulled from every direction. Moments disappear fretted away. Savoring not the delicate morsels of life.

Unburden yourself of publication. Write to write. When writing resembles a cloudy day . . . draw from a palette of human emotions. Experiences real or imagined. Your pen will sing when allowed to flow freely. Paint your manuscript across snow-white paper.

There are as many word combinations as colors to fill the sunset sky. Use the rainbow-colored lyrics of your mind's eye. Give your words life. Let them sing from page to page.

Simply and freely write.

PRAYERS GIFTED FROM COMPASSION

Unity of Hearts

Arrogantly, you remind me. Those are your shoes that trip and stumble in the darkness of pitfalls and suffering. Unique to you, this is true. Compassionately speaking, may I interject? Circumstances vary, but the pain is the same. Extending oneself in times of trouble is the thing to do. Why, if I have suffered would I wish you to do so, too?

Take the hand offered. Receive prayers gifted from compassion, not obligation. It is what makes us human. Even the most courageous may require a sturdy shoulder. In times of need is it as important to give as it is to learn to receive.

It is the unity of hearts that sets us apart from the rest of God's creatures. Take the hand offered in the spirit in which it is gifted. Then, at another time, you may offer to another the strength of a sturdy shoulder.

SMOLDERING ASH OF LIGHT
Flame Eternal

You sit in the nakedness of your humanity. Your vision clouded by the smoldering ash of your Light. A Light, once bold and bright, now snuffed by the actions and ill intentions of others.

Your flame was meant to burn eternal.

Forget the misguided, bad-tempered, and arrogant hiding their nakedness behind the emotional sacrifice of others. Let not the actions of others dim that which you are and that which you can be.

Sit with yourself. List life's expectations. Goals to be reached. Kindhearted missions once accepted.

Live your life in God's Light. Rekindle the fire that burns within. Shine brightly. Shine brightly for the misguided, bad-tempered, and arrogant hiding their nakedness behind the emotional sacrifice for others. They, too, have a flame meant to burn eternal.

SHACKLED MEMORIES
Internal Harmony

You waste countless hours blaming for unrealized life expectations. Award-winning performance as one of life's casualties. Unmanifested desires. Opportunities lost. Shackled to memories and what ifs. My friend, blame not others for your situation. Disappointments come from within. Your hands remain tethered by lack of personal reflection.

Forward progression through life lessons is a necessity for spiritual growth and internal harmony. Sit with yourself. Honest to the point of brutality. Cry tears of acceptance. That was. This is. It no longer need be. Then stand tall in His graces. Pride in yourself for taking ownership and initiating changes.

List goals long-term and immediate. Overwhelming it need not be. Focus on the now instead of the whole. Let the Light shine within. Realized internal bliss.

Forward progression mirrors the strong-willed essence. The reward for painful reflection.

INTEGRITY HONESTY HUMILITY

Riches to Possess

Helplessly I watch as you waste energy traversing life through closed eyes. Bumping into assembled emotional barricades devised to block a broken heart from bad memories. Your self-inflicted obstacle course is keeping you from the true joys of life.

So you focus on acquisition. Flowery, freeze-dried arrangements of pretend happiness. You're gasping for breath. Reaching for life, but your vision remains blurred.

Anxiety lifts only to be replaced. Stressful moments and days. Time drifts. You waste precious life away. Painful memories clog the mind and bind the hands.

You cling to the earthly ladder, a clown hiding behind a painted smile and shallow happiness.

How fragile you are in human form.

Open your eyes. See His Light. Learn to listen while life is still fresh and your mind clear. Waste not on accumulation, but on acceleration. Quickly, change direction. Kind actions, good deeds, and forgiveness. Integrity, honesty, and humility. Learn, listen, and digest. Tear down, then take a breath. Clean air and nature abound. Learn, look, and digest God's blessings.

SURRENDER TO YOUR SORROW

Woundedness

I see the shadowed darkness of your woundedness. Cloaked with insecurities and self-doubt. Sequestered from joyful expressions and opportunities.

You gave love freely but mistakenly to the wrong person. A person more interested in the trinkets of life and immediate gratification. A person consumed with self-indulgent behavior. A person incapable of matching the purity of your love. Are those not *their* deficiencies instead of yours?

Love is more than an emotion. It is the essence of being, programmed into every cell of our body. We fail to thrive without it.

Love in a healthy relationship is matched equally, wholly, and purely. It is more than the bond between lovers. Love is the ability to intimately share and care for another. To tenderly caress their soul with compassion and gentleness. To *see* them for all that they are and all they can be.

Love is not manipulation or exploitation. Love is not needy or greedy. Love is not regimented to a clock or meant to be crammed into a box of opportunity.

Love is the silhouette of God.

Embrace tightly the knowledge that when you are ready, you command the ability to cut the strings that emotionally bind you. You own the strength to forge forward, alone.

You are not to blame. Your love was given deeply, intensely, and innocently.

Surrender to your sorrow.

Tend to your woundedness. In the space of privacy, cry a cleansing cry. Flush away the hurt, anger, disappointment, and pain. Replace it with God's love. Deliberately fill your time with activities until your smile returns, and your sorrow is replaced with joy for a new day.

You are loved. You will find love again. Seek comfort through prayer and God's love.

ONE FOOT FLAT
Spirit of God's Light

Fortunate you are. Minus the negative pulls this way or that. Going in life's direction by the seat of your pants. Planting one foot flat whilst the other meanders. Testing stability. Treading mundanely. Day after day.

Your choice.

Mere existence or make a difference.

A difference made from a footprint in the sand. Rippling effect regardless the action.

Child of God. Warrior of Heaven. You've been gifted this life. You are here with an agenda. Make a difference with your stance. Ripples sent in every direction. Interactions of varying compassion. Gift of yourself. Extension to others. Kind words and actions.

Jump from the bleachered position. Take action. Make a difference.

JOYFUL LIVING

God Gifted

I can't keep up with your revolving life bulletin. Changing comrades and hobbies like a seasonal wardrobe. Unsettled you are with the journey thus far. Reaching to draw from the life of others. Tackling their spirit as your own. Recognizing happiness through their thoughts and actions. Habits then formed. Bored with their life energy . . . then on to another.

Not necessary.

You've been gifted your own.

Create your own goals, memories, and special moments. Unhindered by the intentions, desires, and motivations of others. Comrades and hobbies still you will have. But the life you enjoy will be that of your own. Live the life God has gifted. Fill your calendar with joy and happiness.

When following your own path, straight and clear it will be. Joyfully intersecting comrades and their hobbies, but not directing yours.

Beautiful life . . . just live your own.

GOD'S GIFT
Blessings and Breath

For every action taken or passed, a mark is left upon the sand. The direction, intention, and severity have impact. Close your eyes. Think back.

This is God's place. Numbered he has every grain of sand. Of such importance holds all that He creates.

Gently step with consideration given to all creatures and the soil beneath your feet.

For every choice you make today, a mark is left upon the sand. Step humbly upon the earth. Step firmly with faith. Step in a direction that honors the intention of God when you were gifted breath and the blessings of this day.

VIOLENCE

Take Faith

Violence posted on the airwaves. Violence walking our streets. Violence and hatred spewed across oceans. Violence contagious within nations. Faith, my friend. Take faith.

For scattered amongst the twisted and aggressive litter of humanity sprouts a tender sprig of love and innocence. Found in the heart-place of every human. It is the resting place of God graced to each.

Faith, my friend. Take faith. Regardless your place of worship. We are of the same breath. Children of God.

Focus not on the darkness of heart but instead on *God's Light*. For in the Light each person holds the power to shine. Pray for the unity of hearts. Pray for the graces and blessings of God for all nations. Pray for the sprig of innocence to blossom and flourish. Spreading. Becoming contagious.

Faith and focus. Faith in a world with peace for the seventh generation. Focus on intention. Turn off the darkness by living in Light.

CHALLENGES OF GRIEF
Face another Day

Take heed. This challenging phase will pass. To your knees, you have dropped. Heart in a million pieces. Efforts to stand tall thwarted by the elements. Time wrapped and sealed. Tainted memories splatter the walls. Mirrored curtains reflect scorn. *What ifs* cyclone inside the head. Remnants of self-respect left outside the door. Self-worth scattered to the passing clouds overhead. Grief-ridden tears scream aloud.

Take heed, my friend. This challenging phase will pass. Rise from the cowered position. Ask for help. Sweep a place clean in your heart, for God is near.

Give to God the challenges faced. Give to God space in your heart. Weep no more. All you need to do is ask.

Take heed, my friend. Rock with the movements of the planet and man. Life can and will continue. The sun will rise. Love will find its way. Believe in the healing abilities of prayer. Believe in forgiveness. Believe in the sunrises of tomorrows that follow a peaceful sleep. Believe that happiness will follow grief-filled tears.

Believe, my friend. Believe.

SOCIAL MEDIA AND HEARTBREAK

Great Divide

Heartbreaking when the devices that link us as a people also cause a great divide.

Use the social media to uplift instead of toting a new handbag or bragging about where you went to eat.

Use the social media to link us as children of God instead of political guinea pigs.

Use the social media as a reminder of those who are in need.

Use the social media to reach the homebound.

Use the social media to educate the educated.

Use the social media for the betterment of the whole.

When you see something touching or uplifting, when you see something that touches your heart—please, pass it on. Resend the messages that spread Light. Resend the messages that unite, not divide. Resend the messages that make a difference in a most positive way.

We hold in our hands the device to uplift and link brothers to brothers across open waters and nations. Powerful devices when used in the right way.

WORDS KNOTTED

A Nightingale's Song

Worry not, dear one. The frustration you feel is temporary in nature. Words knotted on the tip of your tongue. Compassionately speaking and nowhere to go. Borrower of words, your command of verse is as a nightingale's song. Gifted the grace to speak to the masses. Heartfelt messages for the many intended. Hearts green to hear.

Your challenge is not the message but patience. Patience with yourself. Patience with the process. The messages will reach those intended. Positive energy gathering momentum. Consoling hearts one dilemma at a time. Guiding with God's Light.

Set free the nightingale's song.

UNFOLDING OF LIFE

Patience Faith Strength

Patience. Faith. Strength. Gods Light.

Unfolding of life, we cannot escape. Events. Health. Relationships. Rough waters. Stormy weather. All will take a toll if navigated alone. Look to God's Light. Find patience, faith, and strength. For through our greatest struggles are the greatest strides made up the spiritual ladder.

Unfolding of life, we cannot escape. How we handle it is what sets us apart. Stand tall in faith. Allow God's Light to shine. Be the example. For in your Light others will follow.

Calm waters ahead.

DEATH'S DARKNESS
Sorrowful Loss

My heart is saddened by your loss. Earth's gentle momentum, suddenly halted. Death's darkness blocks the Light of life. A heart tightly shrouded in cloudy bereavement. Lonely and without peace. Fully you loved. Now frantically clenching precious ribbon-laced memories.

My words cannot heal wounds that weep. The void will cease when you're willing to feel God's healing embrace. Your place on this planet is for a reason. Take refuge in knowing you are fully loved.

My words cannot heal your broken heart. Time, dear one, and love from above.

USED FURNITURE AND CHIPPED PORCELAIN SINKS

Sturdy Stance

Many life experiences you've had, it's true. Exterior rough and worn. Like used furniture and chipped porcelain sinks. Beneath uneven surfaces lies structure of a solid sort. Blemishes of the past enhance the patina called *you*. Sturdy in your stance. Proud and tall. Child of God. An intricate part of the whole.

What better example could there be? With an understanding of the journey's complexities. Each blemish a reminder of a lesson learned. Progression of passion. Service to the whole.

Take pride in humility. Pass each day as an example. The power of prayer. The power of Heaven. Blemishes of the past enhance what you have become. Wear the beauty of knowing the battles fought and won.

Rough life. A term so commonly used. Derogatory in nature. So untrue. There's joy in overcoming the blemishes of life. Look to your patina with pride.

MENDING THE BROKEN HEART
Love and Affection

So fragile it is. The heart so tenderly wrapped and delivered. Swaddled in rose petal sunsets and sacrifices gifted. Only to be torn. Tossed about. Trampled upon. Worn out.

My friend, pull back that which is shattered. Tie together the loose strings of your broken heart. Allow time to mend.

Take care in future situations. Offer next time to a person more deserving. And if your heart should break again. Retie the loose strings knot by knot.

You are deserving of love and affection. You are deserving of positive attention. You deserve all this universe has to offer.

Believe in yourself. Believe in your grandness. Believe in that which God has created. Look to the beauty and worth within. See it. Know it.

Recognize yourself.

JUST PRAY!

Shine Brighter

*P*rayers are not enough. Five or ten minutes taken to adjust mentally. Private in thought. A short flicker of Light and then you're done.

Prayers are enough when laced throughout the day. Accented with good intentions. A virus contagious spreading to the many.

Prayers are enough when united. Sorrowful cries penetrating the skies. Reach out. Hold hands. Hold hearts. We are of the same breath. We share a Father. Unite in prayers regardless of differences. Reach with your heart. Your prayers will take a proper direction.

Prayers are enough to get things going. But don't stop there. Smile. Love. Be happy.

Prayers are enough when the intention is for the whole. The whole of humanity and Earth Mother.

Prayers are enough to shine God's Light and keep the beacon going. Take care with your thoughts. Take care with your intentions. Prayers tucked throughout your day are reminders to shine brighter and brighter.

Pray whist alone. Pray in groups to gather momentum. Pray loudly and proudly.

Just pray.

FAITH AND GOD'S LIGHT
Shadows of Life

Be aware. Darkness exists in the shadows of life. For it stands ready to blanket Light. Clawing and tugging at peaceful intentions. Pocketed within an uncanny awareness of where it resides. Offer no energy. For it survives on anger, fear, and distrust.

Have faith. Eliminate the shadows within. Shine God's Light on the fragments of frailty woven into the human manifest. Face your anger. Face your fear. Face your distrust. Face them with God's Light.

Anger. Fear. Distrust. Shadows of the past. Shadows of humanity. Eliminated by faith and God's Light.

When given a choice . . . look to the Light.

HOME WITH GOD

Flickering Light

You heard it as well. The faint voice. Unveiled from the dark. A bright and shining message of hope, peace, and love.

It is the flickering Light that guides. Cradled within the heart-place when home with God. Utterances barely above a whisper. Gathering momentum. The more you listen, the brighter your life becomes.

Follow the guidance. Follow the Light. Unveil a life magnificent. Use your talents and abilities to lift mankind. Feel and reflect God's Light. It is your birthright. Child of God.

COMPASSION SPOKEN

Lighting the Way

There you go, spreading words to the wind. A one-sided linguist immersed in personal convictions. Wringing your hands because the audience is delinquent. Clarity both a friend and foe. You've awakened, and painfully so. My friend, you cannot control the second half. For when gifting conversation, the other half has a choice to listen.

Worry not for where the words go. To the wind or caught in a raging wave and swooped offshore. Your words will find their place. Decades or distance away.

Wrap your conversations in a heavenly veil. Let them sail on a God-gifted breeze. Tenderly delivered when ready to be heard. Speak boldly through the shadows for those seeking Light. Speak tenderly to the heartbroken drowning in grief. Speak compassionately to the lonely wagering life or death from this moment to the next. Speak often. Speak clearly. Speak from your heart-place. Speak with the voice God has gifted.

There you go, spreading words to the wind. A one-sided linguist immersed in personal convictions. Lighting the way for the suffering. Lifting hearts. Shining ever so brightly in God's Light.

STAND UNITED
Humbled by Grace

Hear the call of hummingbird chatter. Lift up through your actions. Speak clearly with the highest of intentions. Stand united. Arms and hearts extended. Reaching far across nations. Gathering together in the Universe's power.

Significant we are as children of God. Powerful when united. Humbled by God's graces. Harnessing the Universe's power through prayerful connections. Shining brightly. Shining far.

Hear the call. Your talents are needed. Lift up. Speak clearly. Stand united.

PAIN CAREFULLY TENDERED
Cloud of Commotion

Sorry I am for your saddened pace. Wisdom I'll gift from another angle. The decision is for you to make. Let go of the pain you so carefully tender. Tally not over the actions of another. Assume not for the how and why. You may simply be contiguous collateral. Go about your business. Seek joy through the cloud of commotion. The responsibility you must take for personal pleasure.

To the rose garden of life go and plant peace. Water with the simplest of joys and tenderness. Seedlings of forgiveness cultivated. Compassion propagated. Allow others their space to grow. If enlightenment should sprout, forgiveness from *you* they will seek.

Tender your rose garden amidst the commotion. Seek peace.

IMAGINE

Believe

Wedged you are against a wall of indecision. Toes skimming and tripping across uneven pavement. Strength falters. Unable to lift from beneath drama's debris. Circling in concurrent directions. Unable to break free.

My friend, hope is never bottlenecked. It runs freely. Look to the sky to believe. Believe in a future of peaceful existence. Believe in a power greater than you. Believe in your ability to achieve a most beautiful life.

Never are you alone and without. For hope runs through your veins with the power of the Universe. Imagine. Believe.

DEAD-ENDED DECISIONS
Gentle Direction

I watch helplessly from the sidelines of your life. A passage riddled with caverns of your own doing. Paths abandoned. Talents forsaken. Circling through the fog of unsettledness.

If only you could see. Just ahead. Beyond the steepness. A path of beauty. Surrounded in serenity.

I see clearly what your mind blocks out. There—just ahead, dear one. Peace in God's graces. Not my place to push or direct your learning. You must travel at your own pace.

Reminder, I will give. Trust in yourself. Follow the path forward. Listen for direction in the wind. Gentle nudges most lovingly given.

Climb out from the cavern. Rush to the ridge. Look! See what is just beyond. It is within reach. Serenity.

HEALING FORGIVENESS

Life Changing

Time calls. Sunsets pass without notice. The season of age follows. Regardless your social graces or place upon the soil, scattered challenges pebble the path taken. Reflect as far back as you can remember. Stop in this step of forward momentum. Reflect.

Seek forgiveness for hurts you may have caused. Freely offer forgiveness for clashes along the way. For the season of age follows.

Open your heart to the healing graces of forgiveness. Open your heart to God's love.

May the remainder of your journey be peaceful and of the highest integrity. Think before you step. For every step taken intersects with the pebbled path of another.

PASSAGE OF TIME

Holiday Sorrows

You hold in your hand the remnants of a clay holiday pot. Childhood memories lay shattered and scattered. You gather the pieces, but missing is the innocence and purity of youth. How did this happen? When?

My friend, you are trying to put back together something that no longer exists. The passage of time demands the now.

When caught in holiday sorrows—reach out. Call a friend. Call a relative. Volunteer at a shelter. Get out of the house. Do something for someone less fortunate. Keep company with the bell ringer on the corner.

Blessings to you on this holiday season. Prayers I will send to lift up your spirits.

OVERCOME THE PAST
Step into Today

You sit perched upon the ledge of disharmony, teetering within deep emotions. A prisoner of your past, pushing away today and denying yourself of tomorrows. It is an unsettling place to be. A shattered existence. Wishing to disappear from the planet. My friend, the angels grieve for your unnecessary sadness. Leave the shadows in the past.

Come down from the ledge. Step into today. One-step today opens endless possibilities for tomorrow.

Come down from the ledge. God will light the way. Open your heart to the possibilities of a peaceful life with bright tomorrows.

POLITICAL AGENDAS
Times of Challenge

Negativity—negativity—negativity abounds. Threats against the human cause. Political agendas trigger clash amongst neighbors and brothers. Heaviness weighs. The spirit drops.

A challenge, you believe, to be Light at heart.

My friend, more wrong you could not be.

Superficial politics should not replace God. Patience and understanding required. Maintain your balance. Maintain your faith. Faith in yourself and your brethren. Change *is* required. But the change must come from you.

Shine your Light brightly through threats of nature and man. Join hearts and hands with your brothers and sisters through prayer. Your positive energy can make a difference.

Be aware of the shadows, but keep your focus on God's Light.

VIOLENCE AND DRAMA

Prayers to the Universe

We share the same aversion to news events, pop star outfits, and reality show hits. Drama unnecessarily geared sensational. Our world writes a story of its own. Violence and drama on every page.

What if attention was *not* paid to negatives? Gifting them back from where they came.

What if more important were things of a positive nature? Lifting the spirits of the suffering through actions and words of encouragement. Sending prayers to the Universe.

Imagine being tuned in to grand discoveries aiding humankind. Applauding challenges overcome. Documentaries spinning with the goodness still prevalent in the world. What of the day-to-day miracles taken for granted? The butterfly drying flawlessly formed wings. A baby's first breath. A flower in bloom.

When the news is full of positives, I'll tune back in. Until then, I'll continue to focus on the good whilst ignoring the rest.

Acknowledgements

I am forever grateful for my connection with God.

A special thanks to Timothy C. Smith for sharing life's adventures.

To my son, Timothy J. Cassano, thank you for the constant reminder to stretch my vision and abilities.

Thank you to final readers Kathy Scorse, Ernestine B. Colombo, and Janet Thirlby for offering words of encouragement, insights, and reviews.

I would like to thank my publicist, Denise Cassino, for seeing the simplicity of thought and serenity of heart in my verses. Thank you for urging me to publish the three volumes of *Spiritual Verse Today*.

Thank you to Chris O'Byrne and the formatting team from *JETLAUNCH* Book Design for a wonderful experience and fantastic finished product.

A special thanks to Debbie O'Byrne for another amazing cover design.

I am forever grateful for the intersection of your paths with mine.

With warm regards,
—Sharon CassanoLochman

Index

A Miracle Bestowed *Depths of Sadness*, 101
Abandoned at Life's Gate *Dance*, 45
Actions of One *God's Breath*, 94
Anchored to Shore *Facing the Unknown*, 35
Anger Spilling *Peaceful Passage*, 51
Anger Vulnerability Sorrow *Step into God's Light*, 89
Angry Edge *Peace to Your Soul*, 62
Assumptions and Judgements *Shoes of Another*, 74
Attention-Getting Behavior *Good of the Whole*, 113
Awakening *Forgiveness Relieved*, 125
Barnacle upon Her Side *The Earth is Alive*, 29
Battered and Worn *Replacing Strife*, 13
Battle the Page *Let Your Words Bloom*, 110
Battlefields of Life *Comfort in God's Love*, 8
Battles Fought *Peace Deprived*, 116
Believe *Shadow Cast*, 91
Blessed to Call You Friend *Aho*, 11
Blessings Bestowed *Sanction Mind Wanderings*, 9
Borrower of Words *Gifted Talent*, 36

Bottom of the Glass *Believe in Yourself*, 16
Challenges of Grief *Face another Day*, 139
Clover to Buttercups *High Expectations*, 95
Coffee Grounds Spill to the Floor *Ordained Human*, 3
Collective Whole *Whispers in the Wind*, 46
Compassion Spoken *Lighting the Way*, 149
Crooked Choices *Better Tomorrow*, 112
Cruel Host Dementia Plays *Peace and Patience*, 54
Dawn of a New Day *Let Go*, 52
Days Tally *Walk with God*, 75
Dead-Ended Decisions *Gentle Direction*, 153
Death's Darkness *Sorrowful Loss*, 143
Drifting to Monotony *Moments Unknown*, 2
Each Day Forward *Prayer for a Friend*, 32
Earth Day *Cascading the Globe*, 66
Faith and God's Light *Shadows of Life*, 147
Faith *Never Forsaken*, 1
Faithful Life *Judgment Free*, 57
Forgiveness Knot *Live Life Forward*, 76
Forgiveness *Love from a Distance*, 63
Forgotten Sensations *Wakeful Joy*, 69
Found through Plight *Simply You*, 12
Frailty of Heart *Laborer of God*, 121
Friendship Embraced *Purity of Love*, 122
Gifted another Day *Give Gratitude*, 78
Glory of God *Joining of Hearts*, 124
God's Gift *Blessings and Breath*, 137
God's Gift *Second Chances*, 70
God's Gifted Breath *Reconciliation*, 127
God's Voice *Roar of a Wave*, 64
Grace *Smallest of Shoes*, 114
Gratitude to God *Universal Differences*, 31
Grief *God's Light*, 120
Happiness Gifted *Seeker*, 65
Harshly Pointed Fingers *Peace in Your Life*, 33
Healing Forgiveness *Life Changing*, 154

Heart and Soul *Slippery Slope*, 26
Heart Shaken Free *Gifted Awareness*, 40
Heart Still Broken *Delicacy of Life*, 88
Heavenly Chore *Humble Servant*, 21
Heavenly Design *Your Calling*, 73
High Expectations *Stress-Free*, 41
Home with God *Flickering Light*, 148
Honor Life Gifted *Heavenly Connection*, 90
Imagine *Believe*, 152
Integrity Honesty Humility *Riches to Possess*, 132
Joyful Living *God Gifted*, 136
Judgements and Negativities *Goodness of Your Soul*, 5
Just Pray *Peace for All Nations*, 25
Just Pray! *Shine Brighter*, 146
Let Go *Release to God*, 4
Let Your Light Shine *Worthy a Beautiful Life*, 81
Life Eternal *Promised by God*, 92
Life Gifted *Nature's Toll*, 83
Life Lived Full *Laughter Heard*, 104
Limiting Experiences *Extend to Strangers*, 28
Loneliness *Strands of a Web*, 82
Loss of a Perfect Day *Joys of Youth*, 34
Love Gifted *Harm to None*, 68
Measure of Worth *Preacher Teacher Speaker Writer*, 118
Mending the Broken Heart *Love and Affection*, 145
Misplaced Ideals *Grandness of Character*, 67
Mother's Day *Share Bread*, 105
Nearing Journey's End *Compassionate Message*, 18
One Foot Flat *Spirit of God's Light*, 135
Overcome the Past *Step into Today*, 156
Pain Carefully Tendered *Cloud of Commotion*, 151
Passage of Time *Holiday Sorrows*, 155
Path Taken *Heavenly Direction*, 103
Perfection of God's Love *Search Within*, 42
Perfection to Your Core *Breath of God Gave Life*, 23
Personal Connections *Freehand Goodbye*, 22

Political Agendas *Times of Challenge*, 157
Political Persuasion *Spiritual Direction*, 50
Pray for Guidance *Uncertainties of Life*, 58
Prayers Gifted from Compassion *Unity of Hearts*, 129
Ragdoll Enthusiasm *Renew Faith in Yourself*, 20
Raging Anger *Fear Manifested*, 126
Raindrops Haloed *Solid in Faith*, 55
Ravaging Cells *Prayers to You*, 123
Rough Spots Traveled *Patience and Love*, 107
Search with Your Heart *Homeless and Compassion*, 53
Self-Sabotage *Writer's Block*, 48
Set Free *Vivid Colors*, 44
Shackled Memories *Internal Harmony*, 131
Shadows beneath Familiar Faces *White Doves*, 108
Sheltering the Blows *Light against Shore*, 115
Shield of Laughter *Realize Your Worthiness*, 80
Shoes of Another *Spiritual Ladder*, 96
Shroud of Humanity *Courage*, 39
Sing through Words *Rainbow Colored Pages*, 128
Slice of a Sentence *Savor the Flavor*, 59
Smoldering Ash of Light *Flame Eternal*, 130
Social Media and Heartbreak *Great Divide*, 140
Society's Neglect *Heaven's Light*, 97
Spiritual Ladder *Upward Looking*, 87
Stand United *Humbled by Grace*, 150
Stillness of You *Intentions Heard*, 77
Strength of Humanity *Diversity in Light*, 86
Strong in Faith *Life's Gate*, 61
Suffering Souls *Speaking to the Heart*, 6
Surrender to Your Sorrow *Woundedness*, 133
Teetering Direction *Pray*, 106
Tendrils of Goodness *Spreading Gifts of Kindness*, 38
Thorny Path *Healthier Fashion*, 30
Today is for Living *Teapot Screams*, 98
Tormented Existence *Courage to Stand Tall*, 93
Toxic Relationship *Gate Locked and Sealed*, 79

Traffic of Life *Blessings to You*, 117
Troubling Time *Embrace Light*, 71
Twist of Fate *Friendship's Sacred Phase*, 7
Unfolding of Life *Patience Faith Strength*, 142
Universal Suffering *Let God*, 72
Unrelenting Pressure *Exhausting Distraction*, 49
Unsettled Within *God's Embrace*, 85
Unsteady Teeter *Spiritual Journey*, 56
Untidy Your Heart *Release from Sadness*, 14
Used Furniture and Chipped Porcelain Sinks *Sturdy Stance*, 144
Verses Songs Paintings *Spread Goodwill*, 84
Violence and Drama *Prayers to the Universe*, 158
Violence *Take Faith*, 138
Waste Not *Follow God's Light*, 109
Wasted Time *Windows of Life*, 60
Weight of the World *Butterfly Graces*, 100
Weighted Existence *Cleanse*, 111
Words Knotted *A Nightingale's Song*, 141

www.ingramcontent.com/pod-product-compliance
Lightning Source LLC
LaVergne TN
LVHW051833080426
835512LV00018B/2861